WHAT PEOPLE HAVE SAID ABOUT BILLY GRAHAM

I want to pray for Billy Graham and the converts he is reaching. I want to thank God he is succeeding where so many of us have failed.
— LESLIE WEATHERHEAD,
City Temple, London

What is lacking in me and in my theological colleagues in the pulpit and at the university lectern, that makes Billy Graham so necessary?
— HELMUT THIELICKE,
University of Hamburg, Germany

Dr. Graham has taught us all to begin again at the beginning in our evangelism, and speak by the power of the Spirit of sin and righteousness and judgment.
— GEOFFREY LORD FISHER,
Archbishop of Canterbury

Billy Graham is perhaps the most prayed-for man on earth today.
— ARMIN GESSWEIN,
Revival Prayer Fellowship

If the Lord will keep Billy Graham anointed, we'll keep him humble.
— GRADY B. WILSON,
Friend and associate

When the Buddhist priests come into our library, the favorite book they like to borrow is Billy Graham's *Peace with God*.
— CHURCH LIBRARIAN,
Anthong, Thailand

Billy Graham did not influence the evangelical resurgence of our time so much as he epitomized it.
— HAROLD J. OCKENGA,
Pastor, educator

Billy is the most focused man on prayer I ever knew. Each time he called me as a crusade director, he began with, "How's prayer?"

— TOM PHILLIPS,
World missionary leader

Billy Graham is one of those rare jewels who tread this earth periodically and, by their lives and teaching, draw millions of others closer to God.

— MISS RAJKUMARI AMRIT KAUR,
Minister of Health, India

To me Billy Graham is the greatest person to have lived in the twentieth century.

— RICHARD Q. MUSSMAN,
Computer expert

The fall of communism was due to God's will and Billy Graham's preaching.

— GOVERNOR JAMES B. HUNT, JR.,
of North Carolina

Billy Graham can preach in West Berlin where he wants and as long as he wants, your protests notwithstanding.

— MAYOR WILLI BRANDT
(to Mayor Waldemar Schmidt of East Berlin, 1960)

His genius for satisfying a hungry soul is unmatched.

— MARTIN MARTY,
Educator, editor

He does what he says, and has done it since he came to Christ as a teenager.

— MELVIN GRAHAM,
Brother of Billy

I am only a Western Union messenger boy, delivering a telegram from God to the door of humanity.

— BILLY GRAHAM

BILLY

Billy Graham dos Santos, age eleven, stands with his namesake
on the crusade platform before 230,000 Brazilians
in Rio de Janeiro in October 1974.

BILLY

A Personal Look

at Billy Graham,

the World's Best-Loved

Evangelist

~

SHERWOOD ELIOT WIRT

CROSSWAY BOOKS • WHEATON, ILLINOIS
A DIVISION OF GOOD NEWS PUBLISHERS

Billy

Copyright © 1997 by Sherwood Eliot Wirt

Published by Crossway Books
             a division of Good News Publishers
             1300 Crescent Street
             Wheaton, Illinois 60187

Cover photo from the Archives of the Billy Graham Center, Wheaton, Illinois

Cover design: Cindy Kiple

First printing 1997

Printed in the United States of America

ISBN 0-89107-934-3

Scripture verses marked KJV are taken from the King James version.

Scripture verses marked TLB are taken from *The Living Bible* © 1971. Used by permission of Tyndale House Publishers, Inc., Wheaton, IL 60189. All rights reserved.

Unless otherwise designated, Scripture references are taken from the *New King James Version.* Copyright © 1982, Thomas Nelson, Inc., Publishers. Used by permission.

Library of Congress Cataloging-in-Publication Data

Wirt, Sherwood Eliot.
    Billy: a personal look at the world's best-loved evangelist / Sherwood
Eliot Wirt.
        p.   cm.
    Includes bibliographical references and index.
    ISBN 0-89107-934-3 (hardcover: alk. paper)
    1. Graham, Billy, 1918-   .   2. Evangelists—United States—
Biography.   I. Title.
BV3785.G69W48   1997
269'.2'092—dc21   96-40841

05		04		03		02		01		00		99		98		97
15	14	13	12	11	10	9	8	7	6	5	4	3	2		

He put words of hope and joy on people's lips
in the twentieth century.

~

"This was the Lord's doing;
it is marvelous in our eyes."

— Psalm 118:23

To Ruth Bell Graham
poeta, scriptora, filia, uxor, mater, avia—
femina magnifica

～

CONTENTS

FOREWORD

~

Sherwood Eliot Wirt has always rated high on my list of People to Be Watched. He is unpredictable, can believe six impossible things before breakfast, and gets away with audacious utterances. I was intrigued, then, when he told me about this book. Could we entrust Billy Graham to him?

We could, as it happened. Dr. Graham was in safe hands. His approach throughout resembles that of one Scottish Covenanter who said of a colleague, "I could never get my love off that man. I think Jesus Christ has something to do with him."

Right at the outset Dr. Wirt points out that Billy Graham is in human terms inexplicable—much more than the sum of his parts. Wirt promises to tell readers things about the evangelist they may have missed, and he does just that. Here are unique insights and little asides from seventeen years of company-keeping and shared ministry at home and abroad, supplemented from the continuing friendship since Wirt's retirement as editor of *Decision* two decades ago.

In this project he is necessarily selective, averaging four pages for each year of a crowded and eventful life and presenting his observations with infectious enthusiasm. He properly gives credit to the sig-

nificant and sacrificial contributions made to the Billy Graham
Evangelistic Association by team families and by staff members.
When he dons his journalistic hat, I sense Wirt's "sheer hopeless
veracity" (I owe the phrase to Jerome K. Jerome). As an observer on
the sidelines of some of the events he mentions, I hail him as a faithful scribe.

I enjoyed reading this book. It displays generally the whimsical
eccentricity so well known to those who have benefited from his fellowship over the years. He reminds me of that character in *The Little
World of Don Camillo* who said, "I was absurd from the very beginning. Thanks be to God." I mean that in the nicest possible way.

—DR. JAMES D. DOUGLAS,
Author, editor, littérateur

ACKNOWLEDGMENTS

~

This work is neither a biography nor a memoir nor a piece of fiction. It is an attempt to express the esteem in which my colleagues and I hold the amazing man we call our boss. To do so I have had to portray him as I saw him with my own eyes, not just as others have written about him.

The book does include occasional quotations from the writings of Billy's three excellent biographers—Stanley High, John Pollock, and William Martin—as well as from team members, world figures, media folk, and admirers generally of Billy Graham. In every case I have sought to give credit where credit is due.

In expressing appreciation to those who have helped me, I begin with my wife, Ruth Evelyn Wirt, who has lived night and day with the text and who, prior to our marriage in 1987, spent eighteen years as administrative assistant to Leighton Ford and manager of Billy Graham's Canadian office. This is her book too.

The generous cooperation I have received from the staff at Billy Graham's headquarters in Minneapolis, Minnesota, the Billy Graham Center in Wheaton, Illinois, the Billy Graham Training Center at The Cove, Asheville, and at offices in Montreat, North Carolina, as well as from certain individuals has made compiling this volume (my twenty-sixth) a genuine joy. I would mention particularly Stephanie Wills, Billy's secretary; Dr. John Corts, president of the Billy Graham Association; Dr. Roger Palms, editor of *Decision* magazine; Dr. Lois Ferm, BGEA archivist; Robert Shuster, director of the Billy Graham Center archives; Hugh Elder, director at The Cove; Larry Ross, public relations director; and most particularly photographers Russ Busby and Robert Osthus. I thank the critique groups of the San Diego County Christian Writers' Guild, and markedly Mary Jenson, for invaluable help. For help with the Alaska chapter, I am indebted to Dr. Thomas Teply. For technical assistance with my computer, I am grateful to my grandnephew Evan Wirt and to Richard Mussman.

A great many volumes have been written about Billy Graham, and I have consulted a number of them. The libraries of neighboring institutions, particularly Westminster Theological Seminary and Christian Heritage School, have been helpful. The bound volumes of *Decision* magazine, 1960-1996, have been at my disposal, and for that I am grateful to Dr. Roger Palms. I wish to thank my friend Dr. James Dixon Douglas for his percipient foreword. Editors Leonard Goss and Lila Bishop and Publisher Lane Dennis of Crossway Books have been indispensable partners in bringing this book to life.

Many Christian authors dealing with evangelism invite their readers to make a spiritual response to what they have read. If after reading these pages you, friend reader, would like to know more about the Man Christ Jesus whom Billy Graham serves, and whom we serve, I invite you to write me in care of the publisher. You can be sure your letter will be read and answered either by myself or the publisher or by the Graham Association staff.

So now, Billy, here you are as I and many of your friends see you. And we give God all the glory for what He has done in your life, as you do. We're thrilled to have been part of it.

~ MCMAKIN'S CHARGE ~

Scene: A raw pine tabernacle
in Charlotte, North Carolina, November, 1934

Albert McMakin, farmer, sat in the choir,
    his Bible open to Romans seven and eight,
    eyes on the back of Preacher Ham's bald head.
To him the music was the sound of heaven.
He couldn't sing—the boys had sought the loft
    just to evade that bony, pointing finger.
How Albert loved the gospel messages!
A year had passed since Christ first touched his heart,
    and here he was, still eager for discipling
    with two young charges on the plank beside.
He'd put them in the truck and brought them here,
    praying that God might do for them tonight
    what He had done for Albert. Now the choir
    was on its feet; the time of invitation
    was at hand, and Albert and his boys
    stood with the others, mumbling through a tune.
Verse after verse they sang, while Christians prayed
    for wives and sisters, husbands, wayward sons
    and pleasure-minded daughters. "Come to Jesus
    while there's time," cried Mordecai F. Ham,
    and quiet penitents walked slowly down
    the shavings trail to faith and hope and God.
They reached the closing verse when Billy Frank,
    barely sixteen, said something that would change
    the doctrine of the church in Western Europe,
    remove the color bar in Birmingham,
    shorten the Cold War with an early thaw,
    and weld the world's evangelists as one,
    while preaching Christ on every continent.
"I'm going down," he said. Just that. And Grady,
    scion of Walter Wilson, said, "I'm with you."

They teetered on the plank, then walked the steps,
    the tall boy and the chunky one, and stood,
faces upturned at last toward the man,
    while Albert watched and wept and praised the Lord.

— S. E.W.

INTRODUCTION

~

I have talked to many people who have seen Billy on television and heard him speak but who never have had the privilege of meeting him. They tell me they would love to experience the joy of knowing him and catching his warm personality. They would give much to see his smile, hear his laugh, and feel the strong grip of his hand. Year after year Billy Graham is ranked as one of the world's most respected persons, an honor not often accorded to a clergyman. They would like to know for themselves why he commands such respect.

What a beautiful prospect, then, for me to be given the opportunity to write this book about a man who for over half a century has been bringing peace, hope, and joy into the lives of millions of people on six continents and the islands of the sea. It is indeed a pleasure to write about him, though I am deeply conscious of my own inadequacy. But by the grace of God, Billy Graham and I are friends. And so I invite you to meet my friend.

Just about everybody who meets Billy Graham personally becomes aware that there is something very different about him. He is a born leader. It was recognized early by his fellow students when he first enrolled at Wheaton College back in 1941. The difference is not just his appearance nor his voice nor any one particular thing; rather it is the total effect of the man.

What then are the components of this impression? To begin with, Billy is a refined southern gentleman, a compliment to his upbringing and an adornment to his heritage. But before that, he is a Christian and an evangelist. He's not exactly like some evangelists you've known. How can I say it? He is spiritually unique.

For example, he is deadly serious about the devil and the wickedness he continues to cause in the world. Billy is also acutely aware of the burden of suffering that daily afflicts such a large portion of the human race. He has a tender touch. In recent years he and his wife, Ruth, have personally endured their share of affliction. As a global traveler over several decades, he is also keenly sensitive to the tragic injustices existing in the social environment of different nations, including his own.

But all attempts to explain Billy Graham fail unless they begin at the cross. The apostle Paul said, "Christ sent me not to baptize, but to preach the gospel."[1] And what is the Gospel? It is that Christ died on Calvary's cross to save sinners like you and me. It is that He made atonement for sin with His blood, thus redeeming us from hell and judgment, and then gave us the promise of new life in the Holy Spirit by rising from the dead. This is in essence the Christian message, based on the Bible, and it is what Billy preaches all over the world. The message explains the messenger.

But Billy is also a lighthearted individual. Not many realize that. He feels the joy of being alive in God's creation. He is thrilled by the prospects of future bliss in heaven, and he has made a lifetime career of loving God and loving people. That's the note the media fail to catch. They see the hype and the crowds, but they miss the love of the Spirit and the joy of the Lord. They think Billy's story belongs in the "religious" category, along with promotion and hocus-pocus and billboards and sandwich-board prophets and, of course, the money pitch. So they sit down to knock out his story, and it often proves to be a subtle justification for their own sins and a putdown for Billy. It's the blind writers leading the blind readers, and they all end up in the ditch.[2]

But the crowds who show up at the stadium without a press

pass—they get the message from Billy that Christianity is not a religion at all, but a transforming relationship with Jesus Christ. To know Him and be known by Him—that is the way to truth and salvation.

God has given Billy unusual insight into what people are really like. He doesn't believe we are naturally good folks with just some bad tendencies. He believes we are naturally bad, unmistakably bad,[3] thanks to the devil's enticements, but with a great potential in Christ for goodness and mercy. That's what the Bible teaches, and Billy accepts it as God's Word.

The result is that when he preaches, even though he doesn't indulge in eloquent rhetoric, his message from God's Word seems to get inside the listeners. It's as if he is a soul doctor who knows what's going on in our innermost being. Other pulpiteers can and do expound on the exceeding sinfulness of sin; Billy gets downright personal about it. He doesn't condemn us. He just bores in and lets us condemn ourselves.

Without running out a string of clichés, Billy talks about the love of God in Jesus Christ. He stabs the air with his index finger and tells the people, "God is saying to you, 'I love you. I love you. I love you.'" Sitting in the stands, we think, *Man, maybe there's something to this business. The guy rings a bell. Maybe God can tell me what I ought to do about my predicament. My life's a mess. I've got to do something fast. Guess I'll join the others and go down front and check out the Jesus bit.*

Ah, those beautiful crowds that stream forward from all over the stadium at Billy's invitation—what a marvelous sight! There's nothing to match them anywhere on the planet. And it's still going on, decade after decade. Other sincere evangelists reach hundreds; Billy reaches thousands and even millions! A Christian woman member of India's Parliament, Princess Rajkumai Amrid Kaur, said it well back in 1956: "Billy Graham is one of those rare jewels who tread this earth periodically and, by their lives and teaching, draw millions of others closer to God."

Take this harried housewife living in Glasgow, Scotland, who came forward in Kelvin Hall at Billy's invitation to give her heart to

Jesus Christ. Later, when talking to a counselor, she burst into tears. Her husband was a "sore trial" to her, she said, and began going into the details. While she was talking, she heard a voice behind her saying, "Don't worry any more, my dear. I'm here too." Her husband had just accepted Christ and joined her.[4] Her prayer was answered before she even uttered it. That kind of thing is not unusual.

A newspaper received this letter from a subscriber:

> *I write on behalf of my husband and myself. Prior to accepting Billy Graham's call I frankly admit that for many years the word* happiness *was never to be found in our home, owing to continual quarreling between my husband and myself due to excessive drinking. Now our lives are changed in many ways. To attend church was unheard of in our home for years. Now we attend regularly. Happiness prevails in our home. My husband and I thank God for the wonderful change that has taken place in our lives.*[5]

What about Dr. Graham's own morals? We all know the temptations to which those who minister in the name of Christ are exposed. I can begin to answer that by quoting what Billy once said to me: "I am dead to every woman but Ruth!" And what about his participation in popular American social activities? Is he a recluse? No, but here's something else he told me: "I like occasionally to wear a colorful sport jacket, and that's about as wild as I ever get."

Several books have been written over the years criticizing Billy Graham. You ought to read them! You may have trouble locating one, for they are "remaindered" soon after they're published. Actually their contents border on the hilarious because something is missing, and that something is God Himself. Trying to write a book about Billy Graham apart from God is harder than finding the silver dollar that George Washington threw across the Rappahannock River. I don't doubt the authors' sincerity, but I say about their writing what Billy says about a certain California Golden Bear football player. This young man, who was captain-elect, recovered a fumble in the Rose Bowl back in 1929 and ran with the ball the wrong way. He was sincere, but he was sincerely wrong.

This book will take up the question of greatness in relation to Billy Graham. It's not easy, for he insists on giving God a hundred percent of the credit for his success. But in more earthly terms, it's not often that a touch of glory comes our way. It is rarer than Halley's comet; and when it does come, people usually don't recognize it until the person is dead. Then the attacks subside, and the true quality begins to surface. So it will be with Billy for many people.

In the authorized King James Bible appear the words: "Seekest thou great things for thyself? Seek them not."[6]

Billy knows that verse in Jeremiah. Yet the Bible also recognizes that some people are specially anointed of God as His prophets and spokespersons. "Touch not mine anointed," warns the Scripture.[7] And it was Gamaliel, the wise first-century Jewish rabbi, who suggested that the early Christians ought to be left undisturbed, lest their opponents should find themselves fighting against God.[8] He recognized the possibility of glory.

In May 1996, Billy and his wife, Ruth, were awarded a Congressional gold medal by the United States Congress in an unforgettable ceremony in the rotunda of the nation's capitol. It was providential they were there to receive it; so often such recognition of greatness is delayed until it becomes posthumous. More will be said later about that award, as it is another reason for this book.

We who are Billy's friends, who have worked and traveled with him, are keenly aware that there is something special about him, but we also know how human he is. And so were John Chrysostom, Francis of Assisi, Martin Luther, George Whitefield, Abraham Lincoln, Amy Carmichael, and other persons highly regarded by Christians. They were all human, and at the same time they had greatness. The secret is to distinguish the one quality from the other. It's unwise when we ascribe perfection to human beings, all of us being less than perfect. It's unwise to forget that the Spirit of God blows wherever He pleases,[9] and the grace of God works in the axles of the universe without any accountability to us mortals. Only God is perfect.

Billy likes to tell a story about the preacher who said in his sermon one Sunday, "Apart from Christ, there never was a perfect man."

A rustic gentleman in the congregation rose to his feet and interrupted him. "Oh, yes, there was," he drawled.

The preacher raised his eyebrows. "And who might that be, sir?"

"My wife's first husband" was the reply.

To sum up, the special situation of William Franklin Graham II in relation to the famous Christians of history whom we honor is this: At the present writing Billy is here with us now and very much alive. The others have flown away. The question then remains: Is there, indeed, true greatness in our midst? Let the reader decide.

THE
SEED

~

Dear Billy Graham,

Please send me a booklet to study. I'm a christian. I made my cmetmet, Kelly Baker my friend, witnessed to me in my playhouse, we were playing dolls.

Love,

Cassie A. Currie

One

THE HIGH PAGER

~

NOT BY MIGHT NOR BY POWER,
BUT BY MY SPIRIT, SAYS THE LORD.

—ZECHARIAH 4:6

What is spiritual power? Where does it come from? How is it made available?

Contemplate for a moment the work output of Billy Graham in his lifetime—the sermons prepared and preached; the books written; the miles traveled around the globe; the congresses and crusades conducted on every continent; the conferences with world leaders; the demands of an international organization with hundreds of employees and with offices seemingly planted everywhere; the worldwide media exposure and ministry through television, films, and the press; the responsibilities of a home with a wife and large family; the enormous correspondence; the syndicated daily newspaper column; the weekly radio broadcast that reaches around the planet; the oversight of a Christian monthly magazine with the world's largest circulation . . . "and more," as the TV promoters like to say. We are amazed at the sheer work of the man. Conducting such a ministry would tax the strength of a superman, which Graham is not. His own body has paid a heavy price. Yet he is still actively crusading. How does he do it?

We need to understand something that happened to Billy early in his career. As a teenager, he, his biographers note, went forward to receive Jesus Christ at an evangelistic service in North Carolina.

Then, as a student at the Florida Bible Institute, he knelt and sur-
rendered his life afresh on the eighteenth green of a golf course. But
a few years later, he underwent a different kind of spiritual experience.

During his visit to Britain in October 1946, a meeting was
arranged at Hildenborough Hall in Kent where Billy was to be introduced to Christian leaders before his evangelistic tour of cities in
England, Ireland, and Wales. He arrived in time for the closing service of a youth conference, at which the speaker was Stephen Olford.

Olford, born of missionary parents in Angola, had planned to be
an engineer, but a motorcycle accident in England brought him face
to face with God while he was recovering in a hospital. He attended
St. Luke's College and served as World War II chaplain to His
Majesty's Forces, who were leaving for the Dunkirk action. Later he
became an itinerant evangelist.

At Hildenborough Hall Olford preached a fervent message on
the text: "Be not drunk with wine, wherein is excess; but be filled
with the Spirit."[1] When he had finished, he seated himself and rested
his head in his hands. He became aware of someone nearby and
looked up to see Billy Graham standing over him.

"Mr. Olford," said Billy, "I just want to ask you one question:
Why didn't you give an invitation? I would have been the first one to
come forward. You've spoken of something that I don't have. I want
the fullness of the Holy Spirit in my life too."

Billy told his biographer John Pollock, "I was seeking for more
of God in my life, and I felt that here was a man who could help me.
He had a dynamic, a thrill, an exhilaration about him I wanted to
capture."[2]

They arranged to meet in Wales where Billy was scheduled to
preach in a town named Pontypridd, eleven miles from the home of
Olford's parents. In a room in a stone hotel in Pontypridd, Stephen
and Billy spent two days together. Billy told Stephen, "This is serious
business. I have to learn what this is that the Lord has been teaching
you."

The first day was spent, according to Stephen, "on the Word and
on what it really means to expose oneself to the Word in the quiet

time." They spent the hours turning the pages of the Bible, studying passages and verses. Billy prayed, "Lord, I don't want to go on without knowing this anointing You've given my brother."

That night Billy preached to a small crowd. The sermon was "ordinary," according to Stephen, and "not the Welsh kind of preaching." Billy gave an invitation, but the response was sparse.

The next day they met again, and Stephen began concentrating on the work of the Holy Spirit by declaring, "There is no Pentecost without Calvary," and that we "must be broken" like the apostle Paul, who declared himself "crucified with Christ." He then told Billy how God completely turned his life inside out. It was, he said, "an experience of the Holy Spirit in His fullness and anointing." He explained that "where the Spirit is truly Lord over the life, there is liberty, there is release—the sublime freedom of complete submission of oneself in a continuous state of surrender to the indwelling of God's Holy Spirit."

According to Stephen, Billy cried, "Stephen, I see it. That's what I want." His eyes filled with tears—something rare with Billy. It seems he had no appetite that day, only taking a sip of water occasionally. Stephen continued to expound the meaning of the filling of the Spirit in the life of a believer. He said it meant "bowing daily and hourly to the sovereignty of Christ and to the authority of the Word."

From talking and discussing, the two men went to their knees praying and praising. It was about midafternoon on the second day that Billy began pouring out his heart "in a prayer of total dedication to the Lord." According to Stephen, "all heaven broke loose in that dreary little room. It was like Jacob laying hold of God and crying, 'Lord, I will not let Thee go except Thou bless me.'"

They came to a time of rest from prayer. Billy exclaimed, "My heart is so flooded with the Holy Spirit!" They alternately wept and laughed, and Billy began walking back and forth across the room, saying, "I have it! I'm filled. I'm filled. This is the turning point of my life. This will revolutionize my ministry."

Said Olford, "That night Billy was to speak at a large Baptist church nearby. When he rose to preach, he was a man absolutely anointed." Billy's Welsh audience seemed to sense it. They came forward to pray even before the invitation was given. Later when it was given, Olford said, "The Welsh listeners jammed the aisles. There was chaos. Practically the entire audience came rushing forward."

Stephen drove back to his parents' home that night, deeply moved by Billy's new authority and strength. "When I came in the door," he said later, "my father looked at my face and asked, 'What on earth has happened?'

"I sat down at the kitchen table and said, 'Dad, something has happened to Billy Graham. The world is going to hear from this man. He is going to make his mark in history.'"[3] The heavenly reservoir had overflowed.

A close colleague of Billy's before Pontypridd, Chuck Templeton, heard the young preacher after that experience. Astonished, Templeton remarked that Billy's preaching had taken on "a certain magnificence of effect . . . fascinating . . . really impressive."

Speaking in modern terms with a bit of imagination, we might say that for Billy now the High Pager was on. An ordinary pager, such as is carried by thousands of people today, may appear small and even insignificant to the eye, but actually it is loaded with unseen power. It receives signals from a distant point, communicated invisibly and electronically by means of power transmission. Its function is to keep the carrier in touch with home base. This electric signal may operate from a satellite, in which case its range can be international. Ordinarily it operates on a low frequency from a tall tower which, depending on the topography, may be erected on top of a mountain peak. The shining steel towers seen on many skylines could very well be transmitters for pagers.

The analogy holds. The Holy Spirit is simply the High Pager, the invisible, incorruptible, infinite, immortal Source of spiritual power. He pours out the love of God from the heights of heaven into the hearts of believers all over the planet. One might aver that every day from sunrise to midnight, God is "paging" men and women, young and old, rich and poor. He is saying, "Come to me. Hear, and your soul shall live."[4] And using the same analogy, the moment a believer receives God's message and responds by yielding his or her life in complete surrender, the High Pager's switch is open, and the power is on.

That, if I may say so, is what keeps happening to Billy Graham. It is what happens to anyone who enters into communion with Jesus Christ through the Spirit of the living God.

Many people claiming to be "religious" know little or nothing about the Holy Spirit. Some, like the twelve disciples at Ephesus in the apostle Paul's day, have never even heard that there is a Holy Spirit.[5] Such people are easily baffled by the Billy Graham "phenomenon." They look at his attractive person, hear his eloquent voice, are deeply impressed by the adulation of many, including persons of importance, and decide it must be his "personality" that draws people. They try by observation to detect other clues to Billy's greatness. But human qualities do not explain this man's many accomplishments.

Here is the secret: Billy Graham is filled with the Spirit of God. That is the source of his inner power. His life is not so much controlled as invaded by this unseen Source. No matter where he is, no matter what the situation might be in which he finds himself, no matter what his physical condition, he is never more than half a second out of touch with God.

If there is anything special in the makeup of Billy himself, it is an utter lack of pretension. There is no aura about the man. In his spiritual life Billy is not trying to imitate anyone or prove anything or even hint at anything. His behavior is not a pose or an approach or a "thing" he does. The posture of professional holiness is alien to him.

Recently a friend of mine, in company with another Christian gentleman, inadvertently walked into a hotel room where Billy Graham was talking with some church dignitaries. My friend said that Billy walked over and shook hands with them and, after chatting a few moments, said, "It's such a relief to get away from all these big matters and just talk with someone about Jesus!" That's the real Billy.

Many important things about the Third Person of the Trinity are discussed by Dr. Graham in his best-selling book, *The Holy Spirit,* published by Word Books in 1978. He explains that it is when the Holy Spirit has filled a new Christian with God's love that the Christian is enabled to accept the Bible as truth. It is when God's Spirit is communicating clearly that the Christian can believe that God will do what the New Testament says He will do. The Spirit's reservoir of strength and greatness can be drawn upon whenever the High Pager is on.

To the world, believing in the truths and promises of the Bible and seeking to abide by them is "intellectual suicide." To the world, this whole chapter is metaphysical mishmash. The world seeks every avenue to disprove the sacred text, both by argument and by holding it up to withering scorn. But God's ways are not our ways; nor are His thoughts our thoughts,[6] as we shall see.

Two

RESERVOIRS

~

WHO AMONG THE SONS OF THE MIGHTY
CAN BE LIKENED TO THE LORD?

—PSALM 89:6 (KJV)

Growing up in a Christian home on the outskirts of Charlotte, North Carolina, and attending a Bible-centered church with his parents, William Franklin Graham II began his life well instructed from God's Word. Both before and after his decision as a teenager to commit his life to Jesus Christ, godly people surrounded him, and he drank deeply from many springs. We will look at some of them.

Contrary to what one might expect, theological seminary is absent from the list of shaping forces in Billy's life. He never attended seminary. I remember when he came to San Francisco in 1958 and was invited to address students from several seminaries gathered at Berkeley Baptist Divinity School. He was nearing forty, but he told them frankly that they knew a lot more than he did about Christianity. He said he felt "totally inadequate" in their midst. A packed roomful of people did not share the feeling.

I admit freely that I have not known all the tributaries to Billy's spiritual makeup. For example, I did not have the honor of meeting Billy's godly father, W. Frank Graham, whom Billy has called "the finest man I ever knew."

Perhaps foremost in influencing young Graham was his mother, Morrow Graham, a woman of great sweetness of spirit. Brought up on a small vegetable farm outside Charlotte, she was reared to be a Christian and a classic southern lady. She married a dairy farmer and was a devoted wife and the mother of four outstanding children, of whom Billy was the eldest, born November 7, 1918. "Mother" Graham was a dedicated Presbyterian churchwoman and a lot more. Billy often tells how she taught him John 3:16 while she bathed the small boy in a galvanized tub in the family kitchen. In middle life Morrow Graham was introduced by her sister to local Plymouth Brethren views of the Bible, which seem to have added zest, depth, and a touch of glory to her testimony.[1] She became a sought-after Bible instructor and often traveled throughout North Carolina teaching "the branch life" (based on John 15) to groups of praying Christian women.

Ruth Bell Graham, Billy's wife for over half a century, is one of America's favorite role models of womanhood. Her effect on her husband's ministry has been immeasurable. The daughter of a Presbyterian missionary surgeon, she was born in North China and grew up speaking Chinese in several dialects. After attending high school in North Korea, Ruth enrolled at Wheaton College in Illinois, where she met Billy Graham. Marriage two years later in 1943 diverted her from her intended career as a missionary to China or Tibet. As a gracious wife and warmhearted mother of five, she has set an example for the whole world, carrying a heavy load during her husband's extended absences.

Through five decades of marriage Ruth, a dear friend of my late wife, Winola, and myself, has reflected the basic message of Holy Scripture and the principles and values of her father and mother, Dr. and Mrs. Nelson Bell, as well as her own classic southern Presbyterian heritage. Many books have been written about this attractive, charming woman—a poet, author, Bible student and teacher, benefactor, housewife, mother, grandmother, and even humorist.

Dr. Lemuel Nelson Bell, Ruth's distinguished father, served in North China for twenty-five years, until forced to leave his hospital by invading Communists. Returning home to North Carolina, he practiced medicine in Asheville and became executive editor of *Christianity Today*, the magazine his son-in-law founded. An eloquent Bible teacher and fine writer, Dr. Bell was elected moderator of the Presbyterian Church of the U.S. in 1972. He died a year later, shortly after completing his term of office. (More than once this man reminded me that he prayed for me by name each morning.)

Two men at the Florida Bible Institute outside of Tampa where Billy attended for three and a half years also had a great impact on the young student—Dr. W. T. Watson and the Reverend John Minder. Dr. Watson, founder of the Institute, was a Christian and Missionary Alliance preacher with a great vision. Rev. John Minder, the rangy, gentle, godly pastor of the Tampa Gospel Tabernacle, was also an Alliance preacher and served as dean of the Institute. He gave Billy his first preaching opportunities and became a beloved spiritual father to him. Billy ranks him among the strongest influences in his life.

When Billy enrolled in Wheaton College at the age of twenty-one, Dr. V. Raymond Edman was president. Both Billy and Ruth became close friends of Dr. Edman, who was known as "Prexy" to his students. Later when Graham had launched his evangelistic ministry, Dr. Edman often traveled with the team. Billy said of Edman at his homegoing in 1967, "From the day I walked on this campus, his advice and counsel have been a part of my ministry. I never made a major decision without consulting him."

Miss Henrietta Mears, director of Christian education at Hollywood First Presbyterian Church for many years, is credited with sending 400 young men and women into the Christian ministry. In 1949 she invited Billy Graham to address hundreds of students at her August College Briefing Conference. Her friendship and spiritual understanding at that time guided Billy in his decision to build his ministry solely on the Bible. He has called Miss Mears one of the most remarkable Christian women he ever met.

Dr. John Alexander Mackay, president of Princeton Theological Seminary, was one of Billy Graham's strong supporters. He invited Billy to address the seminary's student body and faculty but dissuaded him from taking graduate study. He told Billy he "had already enough intellectual understanding for the work of an evangelist, and if he enrolled as a student, he would find his time being filled in counseling other students."

During his All-Scotland Crusade in 1955, Billy Graham consulted with the Very Reverend James Stuart Stewart, professor of New Testament at New College, University of Edinburgh. The British Broadcasting Corporation had invited Billy to address the entire United Kingdom by television from Kelvin Hall, Glasgow. The subject was to be "The Cross." It would be the first time anywhere in the world to attempt a live telecast of one of his large crusade services.

Professor Stewart's reputation was international. His books of sermons were studied by theologues all over Britain and America. He preached in the great churches of both countries and Canada. On Palm Sunday, at Billy's request, the two men spent a quiet day together discussing the Cross and the Atonement. The professor assured Billy that his position was scriptural, his doctrine was sound and historic, and his understanding of the atonement of Jesus Christ was authentic.

On Good Friday all Britain heard John 3:16 expounded by the American visitor, with people watching in pubs, in tenements, in Buckingham Palace. It was, wrote John Pollock, "the vastest audience addressed by a preacher in Britain . . . second only to the coronation of the Queen." From the Shetland and Orkney Islands in the north to the Isle of Wight, the reception was overwhelmingly positive. An Anglican vicar in Yorkshire wrote Billy that he had been ordained for twenty years and had finally, after a lifetime of searching, found Christ during the telecast. One year later an invitation came to the American evangelist from Windsor Castle.

In this chapter we have been speaking of reservoirs of influence in human terms. The plain fact is that the ministry of Billy Graham defies all attempts at explanation on a human level. Billy is God's man. He is neither mystic nor ascetic "holy man" nor minor divinity, as the world understands such terms. There is nothing either magical or purely psychological in the way people respond to his preaching.

The reservoirs we have described were deep. They helped Billy Graham build in our lifetime a ministry that has changed the way Christians look at evangelism. They also enabled him to bring a whiff of divinity into the second half of the twentieth century.

Three

CHALLENGE AND RESPONSE

~

Whoso has felt the Spirit of the Highest,
Cannot confound nor doubt Him nor deny:
Yea with one voice, O world, tho' thou deniest,
Stand thou on that side, for on this am I.
—FREDERIC W. H. MYERS, SAINT PAUL

I RUN STRAIGHT TO THE GOAL.
—1 CORINTHIANS 9:26 (TLB)

In the summer of 1949 a momentous hour came when Billy Graham drew on his Lord for what he called "a lasting, unassailable strength." The spiritual crisis he faced put his future in jeopardy. The issue at stake was ostensibly the integrity of the Bible, but in reality it was the authority of the Holy Spirit of God. Billy has often spoken about the situation that arose, and his biographers have discussed it at length.

I did not know Billy in 1949, so I was quite unaware of what he was going through, but I did have a couple of encounters with one of the other persons directly involved.

Charles Templeton, who was and still is Billy's friend, grew up in a broken home, his father having deserted the family. But Charles developed into a tall, handsome, intellectually acute young man. As a budding preacher in the Nazarene church, he won considerable acclaim and was chosen to direct the newly formed Toronto Youth for Christ.

Billy Graham, after his marriage, accepted a call to pastor a Baptist church in Western Springs, Illinois. With singer George

Beverly Shea, he developed a popular radio ministry in nearby Chicago. He became friends with Torrey Johnson, who had organized Chicagoland Youth for Christ and now was planning to form a Youth for Christ International, with himself as president. For vice presidents Torrey chose Chuck Templeton and Billy Graham. The three men, with two other Christians, paid an evangelistic visit to Europe. Billy was then named Youth for Christ's first full-time evangelist. It was Templeton who proposed the motion to the young board to elect him. He and Billy had become good friends.

As a result of the election, Billy Graham resigned his pastorate and began to travel. He has never stopped.

People who knew Templeton during his Toronto days have told me that long before he joined Youth for Christ International, he had spiritual problems and was showing indications of restlessness. He has informed Billy's biographers that he became increasingly aware of how easy it was to manipulate people from the pulpit. It seems that religious phrases rolled smoothly off his lips. He complained to Billy that their motivation was not all spiritual, that a lot of their success could be attributed simply to "animal magnetism."[1] Frequently he criticized what he described as the "glibness" and "facileness" of Youth for Christ evangelism.

In 1948 Templeton applied to Princeton Theological Seminary for admission as a student. He was accepted despite his academic deficiencies. At the time he urged Billy Graham to return to seminary with him, pointing out that they were facing unexplained problems in the Bible. He said he felt the need to undergird his own ministry with a broader understanding of the faith.

Billy greatly admired Chuck, but such talk was disturbing. To him the Bible was God's holy Word. At Florida Bible Institute and Wheaton College the Bible had not been challenged; rather it was revered and reinforced. Billy said to Chuck, "Wiser men than you or I will ever be have already encountered and examined all your arguments, and they have concluded that the biblical record can be completely trusted."

In researching this story, I couldn't help thinking about the old "puffing parson" in John Masefield's poem, "The Everlasting

Mercy." The young rebel in the poem, Saul Kane, angrily taunted the parson for trusting the Holy Scriptures, whereupon the parson made his gentle response:

> *The Bible is a lie, say you,*
> *Where do you stand, suppose it true?*

But Templeton's thinking had proceeded beyond attacking the Bible; he was now questioning the very existence of God Himself.

In 1947 Henrietta Mears invited Billy to take part in the College Briefing Conference she conducted at the Forest Home Conference Grounds in California's San Bernardino Mountains. Chuck Templeton, who was still regarded as a leading evangelist, was also invited to be on the faculty.

In the discussions that took place between the two men at Forest Home, Templeton challenged Billy to "use his mind" in approaching the problems of Scripture. But the issue went deeper than a debate over words.

Later, wandering alone among the pine trees, Billy resisted the challenge of intellectual doubt. He did so just as our Lord resisted the temptations of Satan in the wilderness, as Martin Luther resisted the Holy Roman Emperor at the Diet of Worms, as Charles Spurgeon resisted the English Baptist leadership in the nineteenth-century "downgrade" controversy, as Pastor Martin Niemöller resisted the "German theology" heresy of the Nazi leadership, and as Pastor Wang Ming Tao resisted the indoctrination of the Chinese Communists who demanded that he deny the kingship of Jesus.

Clearly the real issue involved in the controversy at Forest Home did not surface at the time. It was the lordship of the triune God Himself, who said, "I will not give My glory to another." But is God really God? Is He a God of love and power, of truth and wisdom, of justice and holiness, of mercy and salvation and joy? Does He care about humanity? Does He hear and answer prayer? Is Jesus Christ really God the Son? Does He equip men and women with supernatural grace and favor when they seek His face and place their lives at His disposal? Does God fill us with the Holy Spirit and visit us in hidden and unseen ways when we defy the pattern of the world and commit ourselves to His own pattern of crucifixion and resurrection? These were the real questions at issue for Billy. They are always the questions at the back of biblical controversy.

Henrietta Mears was a great spiritual reservoir for Billy in those few days. He also spent hours alone—walking, thinking, trying to make up his mind. For Billy it was a critical hour, humanly speaking; but from the mighty crags and palisades that surround Forest Home, God's Spirit began speaking to his soul. Billy told his biographer John Pollock, "I got my Bible and went out in the moonlight, and I came to a stump. I placed my Bible on the stump and knelt down and said, 'Oh, God, I cannot answer some of the questions Chuck and some of the other people are raising, but I accept this book by faith as the Word of God.'"[2]

Since those mountain moments Billy has often repeated that "when I preach the Bible straight—no questions, no doubts, no hesitations—then God gives me a power that's beyond me. When I say, 'The Bible says,' God gives me this incredible power. It's something I don't completely understand." He adds, "When I pick up the Bible, I feel as though I have a rapier in my hands."

Leaving Forest Home behind, Billy drove to Washington Boulevard and Hill street in Los Angeles. What started there in September 1949 as a modest series of tent meetings organized by conservative-minded, praying Christians erupted within weeks into an awakening of human souls that in the fullness of time shook the world until its spiritual teeth rattled.

And what happened to Mr. Templeton? On the surface, nothing. He remained handsome, detached, charming, brilliant, moving among the centers of ecclesiastical power with aplomb. He became director of evangelism for the National Council of Churches, and later for the United Presbyterian Church, U.S.A.

I saw Templeton perform twice in later years, once in 1952 and again in 1954, during his visits to California. He was still called an evangelist. While I knew little about him and had no idea of his relationship to Billy Graham, I remember having a negative impression after hearing him speak. Soon afterward he left the church and publicly renounced his faith. Today there are Christians in Canada, where Templeton lives in retirement, who still maintain their warm friendship with him and pray for his soul. So does Billy Graham.

Today, after a lifetime of preaching, Billy is facing a social order in which the media daily proclaim that Christianity in the West is losing ground. The God of Abraham, Isaac, and Jacob is being challenged by other gods. The sacredness of marriage is being threatened by unnatural practices that are winning sanction. The courts are abandoning any notion of a higher law than the laws they write. Good and evil, right and wrong are regarded as relative, not absolute. Everyone now has "the right to define one's own concept of existence, of meaning of the universe, and of the mystery of human life." Stalin's dictum, "there is no such thing as eternal truth," has gained acceptance. The only certainly left is uncertainty, and as a result, our youth are growing up without a clue as to what life is about.

But are things really that bad? Yes, they are. My mother-in-law, who led me to Christ, used to remark after reading someone's boast in the press about scientific progress, "Let God be true but every man a liar."[3] The signs of social deterioration continue to form the backdrop to Billy Graham's preaching just as similar signs evoked the prophecy in Isaiah 1. The New Testament predicts that conditions will grow worse, not better.

The story is told of a very ancient inscription found carved on a buried stone in Iraq. When deciphered from the Sumerian script, it read: "Everything is falling apart. God has forgotten us. Invasion is imminent. Taxes are intolerable. The drought has destroyed our crops. Lawlessness is increasing. The roads are not safe. Children no longer obey their parents. And everyone wants to write a book!"

A case may be made to show that things have always been bad, that history is nothing but *deja vu*. It's pretty obvious that some things keep recurring and other things simply wear out. The idol worship of ancient Egypt, Assyria, Greece, Canaan, and Philistia came and went. The religions of Manichaeism, Mithraism, and Pelagianism, once so popular in the Mediterranean world—where are they? The difficulty is that Satan is still with us and will remain active until the sacred prophecies are fulfilled. Meanwhile sin and ungodliness have taken new forms, and New Age cults and theological aberrations such as the pretentious "Jesus Seminar" turn out to be no more than ancient heresies in a new format.

The joy of Billy Graham's Gospel is that he is on the winning side. Like the great soul-winners and revivalists of another day, he presents simply and clearly the truth that Jesus Christ died for our sins on the cross of Calvary and is alive today. The Carpenter of Nazareth has risen from the grave and has sent His Holy Spirit into the world with a message of redemption and eternal life.

For nearly five decades Billy Graham has proclaimed those glad tidings of great joy to millions of people. In doing so he has helped bring evangelicalism out from the "Protestant underground," as it was sometimes called. He gave the Gospel credibility in the halls of state and even in the Kremlin. He lit a spark, and the spark caught fire. It is not Christian to compare Billy's work with the work of other evangelists, but we can surely say that he was and is a most unusual man of God.

Today the Holy Spirit is active in a fresh way in churches and home fellowships all over the surface of the planet,[4] and neither Billy Graham nor anybody else seeks to claim the credit. All the glory goes to God. And no church can claim the Holy Spirit for its own to the exclusion of other churches, for the Spirit is free as the wind. He is truth, and truth can be found everywhere. He is love, and love knows no boundaries. He is joy and power and riches and wisdom and grace and honor and blessing, and these are greater than the universe itself because they are the attributes of the living God.

What a wonderful time to be alive, when churches are loosening up, and worshipers are smiling and leaving their neckties at home and lifting their hands in prayer. What a wonderful day when God's servant Billy Graham and others like him around the world are still proclaiming the Good News, and sinners such as you and I once were are still responding, and the Holy Spirit is still equipping new converts to "go and do likewise." *Soli Deo gloria.*

Four

BILLY WHO?

~

CALL TO ME, AND I WILL ANSWER YOU, AND SHOW YOU GREAT
AND MIGHTY THINGS, WHICH YOU DO NOT KNOW.

—JEREMIAH 33:3

L et us pay a quick visit to that borrowed tent on the vacant lot at
Washington Boulevard and Hill Street in the city of Los Angeles
in the year 1949. Inside are the folding seats, two of which are
reserved for us. This eloquent young man from North Carolina has
opened his Bible and is preparing to step to the podium when George
Beverly Shea stops singing. Thousands of listeners have filled the tent.
In an adjoining tent other thousands are on their knees praying fer-
vently for the speaker and his listeners.[1]

Now I invite you to allow your imagination to roam. Let's
assume that in the vaults of heaven a vast choir of angels is also listening to the music of Tedd Smith's piano. A faint sound emanates
from Earth, known widely in celestial circles as the Planet of Discord.
Heavenly applause breaks out as singing now rises from the tent and
blends harmoniously with the eternal music of the spheres: "To God
be the glory, great things He has done!"

Does all this sound a bit euphoric? Not to a believer. Try to
understand. Music is the first thing a new believer hears when he or
she enters the everlasting doors of the kingdom of God. As for Billy
Graham, he is an ordinary man except for this one thing. He is a citizen of the heavenly kingdom as well as of the United States of

America. He lives with his God as well as with his wife and family. God makes him extraordinary. Thus my writing about Billy Graham is not like other biographical works on the man. My intent is not to evaluate, but to render a tribute if I can, and to say what millions of Billy's friends around the world would like to say if they could. I can't explain it further except to say that I sense angels are listening.

When the Greater Los Angeles Crusade for Christ was coming to a close, I was 7,000 miles away, sitting down to a sparse Thanksgiving dinner in a north Morningside flat in Edinburgh, Scotland. My hosts were Helen Forde, a charming widow visiting from Santa Monica, California, and her son-in-law and daughter, the Reverend and Mrs. Frederick Woodward of Virginia.

Our American Thanksgiving Day is not, of course, observed in Scotland, and in that postwar period we were still restricted by British "austerity" (too often sans meat, sans milk, sans eggs, sans petrol). Still the table was bountiful in its Scottish way, and we had so much for which to render thanks to our God. Frederick and I were graduate students in the New College at that athenaeum of learning and wisdom, the world-famous University of Edinburgh.

While we worked our way through the sausage skins stuffed with meal, Mrs. Forde said to me as a fellow Californian, "Isn't it wonderful how God has been using Billy Graham back home?"

I expressed a polite interest. "Billy who?"

"Billy Graham. You know, the young evangelist from North Carolina."

I didn't know. I was currently trying to improve my German by reading Rudolf Bultmann's ponderous treatise on demythologizing the New Testament. "Tell me about him."

"He has been preaching the Gospel in a tent, and thousands are coming forward to be saved. They say he's a Baptist. I'm not sure, but I went there and watched. It was like a revival. Beautiful!"

"You mean in L.A.?" I asked, reaching for a cluster of Algerian grapes. "Who is he?"

Five years passed. By 1954 I had returned to California and was pastoring a rather miniscule congregation in south Berkeley across the bay from San Francisco when I received an invitation to watch a film at a nearby church. The film was a ten-minute newsreel depicting Billy Graham's arrival in London, England, to open his twelve-week evangelistic crusade in Harringay Arena on March 1, 1954.

I had been reading in Christian publications about those packed-out meetings in the arena and particularly about the hostile London press that greeted him with, "Who invited you over here anyway? Do you think you can save Britain?"

One unusually harsh critic, William Conner, wrote two attacks in the *Daily Mirror* under the name of "Cassandra." Billy in turn wrote him a complimentary letter, asking for an interview.

"Will you," Cassandra responded, "meet someone fairly hell-bent and not averse to a little quiet wickedness? Why should we not meet in a pub called The Baptist's Head? You could drink what you choose while I sin quietly with a little beer."

It seems they met, and afterward Cassandra wrote:

> He came into The Baptist's Head absolutely at home—a tee-totaler and an abstainer able to make himself completely at ease in the spit and sawdust department, a difficult thing to do. He has a kind of ferocious cordiality that scares ordinary sinners stone-cold. I never thought that friendliness had such a sharp cutting edge. I never thought that simplicity could cudgel us sinners so . . . hard. We live and learn. The bloke means everything he says. And in this country he has been welcomed with an exuberance that makes us blush behind our precious Anglo-Saxon reserve.

At the final overflowing Friday night service in Harringay Arena, Cassandra was there.

All of this publicity made me, as an old reporter, extremely impatient to see that film. But as I sat there for those ten or twelve minutes, what inspired me during the film showing, and still inspires me, was not so much the huge welcoming crowd that greeted Billy and his team in the Waterloo railway station. Nor was it the jubilant, receptive audiences that packed the Harringay Arena "full and running over" night after night. Rather it was a simple statement Billy made to a congregation in one of the London churches on his arrival.

Obviously responding to the vitriolic criticism in the metropolitan London press, Billy told the assembled people, "We have not come here to save you. We have not come to reform you. We have come at the invitation of the churches of London to preach the unsearchable riches of Jesus Christ to the people of Britain."

Billy then quoted two verses that put a brand on my soul. The first was from Psalm 27:8: "When You said, 'Seek My face,' My heart said to You, 'Your face, Lord, I will seek.'" The other was taken from Jeremiah 29:13: "And you will seek Me and find Me, when you search for Me with all your heart."

Those words forced me into what the sports writers call an "agonizing reappraisal." Things were not going well in my life, either domestically or vocationally, and I knew it. Small as my church was, it was wearing me out. The youth work was faltering. The organist was deaf. People liked me all right, but they gently resisted my ideas, some of which should have been resisted. The neighborhood was changing. People were moving away. The harder I tried to resist the tide, the more I suffered from battle fatigue. Yet I was aware in my heart that if I could find God, if I could earnestly seek God's face and be found by Him, nothing else mattered.

It was obvious that I was not having a very effective ministry among my congregation. Such gifts as I had were limited, and questions about the Bible continued to harass me. But beyond all personal matters, I possessed a vast impatience with the ministry itself. With all its interminable duties, it seemed I just wasn't doing anything. But in that film I had watched people singing joyful Christian songs with tremendous zeal as they rode the London underground to Harringay. (The London *Daily Telegraph* reported: "The tube trains are packed with these singing multitudes."[2]) I couldn't even get my people to sing in church!

Jealousy was not my problem; I bore no ill will whatever toward Billy Graham or any other preacher of the Gospel. What I felt was entirely personal, and it went deep. Jesus said He came to set us free, but I seemed to be locked into an ecclesiastical establishment that made me feel that I was outside the stream of life, answering questions no one was asking, performing traditional religious duties of insignificance to God or humanity. I was like a windup toy that needed winding. While I loved the church of God and wanted to see it prosper, I despaired of my place in it.

Now the amazing scenes in that ten-minute film brought me up short. It appeared that the church's message about Jesus Christ really was relevant to lots of people, even to those who didn't go to church. The London *Daily Mail* was saying about Billy, "He has no magic, no magnetism; he makes no appeal to the emotions. His power—and power he has—is in his indivisible conviction that he knows the right way of life."[3] *Perhaps*, I thought, *if I couldn't reach anybody for God myself, I might get behind somebody who could. But first I had better unkink my theology, quit reading Reinhold Niebuhr, and start praying for Billy Graham.*

Later that year Billy Graham, now clearly a mature evangelist with an international reputation, paid a brief visit to major cities along the Pacific coast. He conferred with committees of ministers and laymen about future crusades and spoke at evening rallies. When he came to the Bay Area, he was invited to preach at a one-night rally in San Francisco's Civic Auditorium.

During the five years that had elapsed since I first heard Mrs. Forde speak of Billy, my enthusiasm had been mounting about what he was doing. I had followed reports of his ministry in New England, in Portland, Oregon, in Seattle, in Minneapolis, Pittsburgh, and some of the southern cities.

In the summer of 1954, while I was on a solo hike in the high Sierras, God had convinced me that His Bible is infallible. As a colleague of mine liked to put it, I "strangled my intellect." Whatever it was God did or I did, my ministry took off in a new direction. I altered my pulpit message and joined a group of praying pastors. So when I read about the coming rally in San Francisco, I gladly filled my car with parishioners on a November evening and took them across the bay to hear the evangelist.

Knowing that San Francisco at night in November could be cold, damp, and windy, I wore a thick Harris tweed suit I had purchased in Edinburgh. Sure enough, at the entrance to the Civic Auditorium a waiting line extended for two long blocks. We stood shivering until some ushers came along to cheer us. When they learned that I was a minister, they invited me inside to sit with a hundred other pastors on the platform behind the podium. During the service Cliff Barrows called on us to stand and sing together, "Standing on the Promises of Christ My King." I sang my heart out.

What amazed me that night was the lighthearted spirit of the audience. It was exactly like what I had witnessed in that London film—a kind of Christian party. Expressions of joy were everywhere. Cliff Barrows seemed full of contagious good cheer as he led the singing. How different it was from the dignified religious solemnity I was used to—which meant, I was taught, doing things correctly, i.e., "decently and in order."[4]

When Billy came to the platform, he too seemed to convey a light spirit. He was the essence of cordiality until he began to preach. His text was the story of the rich young ruler and Jesus, as found in Luke 18:18-24. In sharp, rapid, effective sentences he presented the Bible scene. This young man, he said, was searching for answers at the right time (in his youth). He came with the right attitude (running) to the right person (Jesus). He asked Jesus the right question (about gaining eternal life) and received the right answer (sell what you have; give to the poor; take up your cross and follow Me). Then, said Billy, he did the wrong thing.

It was a well-constructed message, and I found it vivid and electrifying. The preacher was tall, lean, vigorous, impressive. He modulated his voice well; he pointed a long finger, swung his body, flexed his arms, and held up his Bible. His blue eyes were piercing, and his words were sharp, rapid, and effective. His southern accent sounded a bit odd to us Californians when he pronounced "can't" as "cain't," but nobody seemed to mind. The response was impressive as hundreds of people came to the front at his invitation.

At the close of the service, I left the platform to collect my carload of passengers for the trip across the Bay Bridge. They were missing. All had gone forward to give their lives to Jesus Christ.

Five

THE CITY

~

I WILL SHOW THEM MARVELOUS THINGS.
—MICAH 7:15

God loves this rebel city,
loves foemen brisk and game.
—VACHEL LINDSAY
(FROM "THE CITY THAT WOULD NOT REPENT")[1]

I cannot write feelingly about Billy Graham's magnificent sixteen weeks of ministry in New York City in 1957 because, unfortunately, I was not there. Our family had moved from south Berkeley, California, to east Oakland, where I was now having a rewarding time pastoring a lively church and watching God at work.

Ever since I had begun preaching the Bible as God's authentic, inerrant Word, my ministerial frustrations had diminished. Many things in my life had come out of the shadows and into the sunshine, though there were dark patches still.

Now the word was circulating among the churches that Billy Graham was coming back to San Francisco, the city that poet Vachel Lindsay said "would not repent," to conduct a four-week crusade in the famed Cow Palace, beginning in April 1958.

A number of us ministers had been praying for it and expecting it. Charlie Riggs of the Graham team had given me a list of East Bay churches interested in joining the crusade. I was contacting them and arranging for late-night prayer meetings after the regular Wednesday evening prayer hour—to pray for Billy to come to San Francisco. I went to a lot of those prayer meetings myself.

In recent years I had been reading J. Edwin Orr and W. W. Sweet about the great revivals of history. In one particular book published in 1904, titled *Great Revivals and the Great Republic,* I found this startling statement by Warren Candler, a bishop of the Methodist Episcopal Church, South:

> The next great awakening will . . . bring forth . . . mighty men of God [who] will do something more than stir a local interest or excite a transient enthusiasm. Aided by all the modern devices of transportation and communication, they will be able to extend their influence as the revivalists in former times could not. . . . In America we may reasonably expect a great revival, the center of which will be in the west, and the power of which will be felt all along the Pacific Coast.[2]

In the fall of 1957 I put together a little booklet called "Spiritual Awakening," and it was published by Cowman Press of Los Angeles. I quoted Bishop Candler's words. The publisher, Floyd Thatcher, sent a copy to Billy Graham and also one to Carl Henry at *Christianity Today*. The next thing I knew, Billy Graham was quoting Bishop Candler on his national radio broadcast, *The Hour of Decision,* and Carl Henry was inviting me to cover Billy's San Francisco crusade for his magazine!

I continued to visit other evangelical churches in the East Bay, urging them to conduct special late-night prayer sessions on Wednesday evenings to intercede for Billy Graham. All this was unknown to the crusade committee, which was busy with other preparations. On Wednesday nights I found a lot of prayer warriors keen for revival, hoping God would bring it through Billy Graham. It was a time of glorious anticipation.

I had grown up in Berkeley on the eastern shore of San Francisco Bay. Before the bridges were built, the Berkeley I knew was a quiet, scholarly bedroom community from which thousands of businessmen, including my own father, commuted daily by electric train and ferryboat to "the city."

I knew San Francisco. Boy, did I know it! For decades it had boasted a colorful history and sophisticated reputation. As a cocky sophomore at the University of California, I had dropped my Eagle Scout outlook and moved into the fast lane. That included touring Europe with a glee club and dancing with sorority coeds (wearing two-dollar gardenia corsages) at San Francisco's Fairmont, St. Francis, and Mark Hopkins hotels. Later I worked in a Mission Street factory and spent a year as a news reporter on the San Francisco *Examiner*, reporting fires, football, and fifty-seven varieties of sin.

Those were the thirties. Now we were in the fifties; I was wedded to a Christian girl whose mother owned a Scofield Bible, and you know how those things go! I had changed a lot, but in April 1958, I doubted whether San Francisco had changed at all. Vachel Lindsay's "golden leopard" was as unrepentant as ever.

A welcoming party met Dr. Graham at the Southern Pacific train depot, and they drove to the Hotel Californian. There in a small suite overlooking the skyscrapers, Billy held a press conference. The reporters were waiting for him. Coffee was served. I shook hands with Billy's father-in-law, Dr. Nelson Bell, executive editor of *Christianity Today*; with the crusade director, Dr. Walter Smyth; and with Billy.

The greetings were so cordial, the atmosphere so warm and congenial, that I was not only captivated—I felt ecstatic. God had brought me into the presence of some people through whom He was actually doing something. I couldn't believe it. Even the reporters' questions reflected the upbeat atmosphere. I remembered that a few weeks earlier when the Reverend James Pike arrived to become the new bishop of San Francisco, he ordered two cases of whiskey for his press reception. But here the reporters were in a different mood, talking in a different vein to a different kind of reverend about the unseen mysteries of life—about sin and salvation and the very existence of the great God Himself!

And what did Billy tell them at that conference? That the whole nation needed an awakening, and it might well start here. That he was not saying San Francisco was more sinful than other cities. That he was not preaching sectarianism and was not trying to make

Baptists of everybody. That the basic problem of society was not the H-bomb or the guided missile threat but the human heart.

The church editor of the prestigious San Francisco *Chronicle* was among those present. She was a lapsed member of the Armenian Orthodox church into which she had been born. Later, when we got to know each other, she told me that on that first day while Billy was answering questions in the hotel room, she felt herself suddenly swept into the kingdom of God, born again of the Holy Spirit.

The following day, Sunday, April 27, the crusade was to open. My wife, our son, my mother-in-law, her sister, and I filled the car. Once over the Bay Bridge and on the Bayshore Freeway, I turned off too soon. Realizing my mistake (but not admitting it), I circled around to the Cow Palace and found a convenient parking place. When Cliff Barrows stepped to the podium at three o'clock, we were inside, comfortable in good seats.

Cliff's first announcement was that traffic bound for the crusade was backed up for six miles on the Bayshore Freeway. Most of those people never got there that day. Did I make a mistake when I turned off early, or is there a God in heaven? Inside the building 18,000 people were sitting and standing, while 5,000 more waited outside, unable to get in. A choir of 1,500 voices, recruited from churches all over the Bay Area, began singing "Blessed Assurance." The people joined in. Billy went outside to invite those 5,000 standing at the gate, not to come inside, but to come to Christ. Hundreds raised their hands. On the way back to the pulpit, he paused to pray at the side of a paralyzed woman lying in an iron lung.

The musical service proceeded, people were introduced, George Beverly Shea sang, and Billy Graham opened his Bible. One word was often used to describe what happened at that gathering in the Cow Palace of San Francisco on that Sunday afternoon. The word was *awesome,* but on reflection I would say a better word for it would be *joyous.* Billy Graham based his message on a stern passage in the prophecy of Isaiah, but it only reinforced the jubilant spirit of the crowd.[3]

When at the close of his message he extended the gospel invitation, people rose from their seats and streamed forward to commit their lives to the Savior, many of them weeping tears of gladness. They were the first of the 28,254 who responded during the seven weeks of Billy's preaching.

And that was only the immediate scene. Nearly every city in Australia had a Graham prayer group praying for the meetings in California. Bob Pierce reported that Soviet Christians in Kiev and Moscow were praying for San Francisco. In India, Germany, and Taiwan it was the same story. Around the shores of San Francisco Bay 1,200 cottage prayer groups gathered weekly, asking God to bless the meetings.

The people at Hillside Church, where I was pastor, had early caught the enthusiasm generated from the pulpit. Dr. Smyth, the crusade director, came and preached to us and prayed for a "heaven-sent revival." Meanwhile three other local pastors joined me in chartering a bus that offered free rides nightly from east Oakland over the Bay Bridge to the Cow Palace. Our youth group, our choir, our elders, and our prayer warriors all became zealous members of the nightly audience. The bus driver was an early convert.

I have always been dissatisfied with the spectator status of a reporter who never does anything but only writes about what other people do. One night forty-two of our Hillside young people drove across the bridge to the crusade. When Billy gave his invitation, thirty-one of them went forward. I had already seen some members of our choir and even one or two of our elders down at the altar, but this was too much. Our Hillside kids at the Cow Palace altar giving their lives to Jesus?

I went to Lorne Sanny, the Navigator president, who was heading the counseling and follow-up activity, and reported for work. He took off my press badge and gave me a counseling badge (I had already taken the course). For the next few nights I stayed late, talking and praying with inquirers in an overflow room and getting blessed out.

Each evening before stepping on the platform, Billy held a brief press conference in a small dressing room at the Cow Palace. As the holder of a press pass, I attended frequently, sitting quietly in the back row. I thought Billy was unaware of my presence until one night he spoke to me.

"Do you have a Ph.D.?" he asked.

Surprised, I replied, "Yes, sir."

"Where?"

"Edinburgh University."

"I always admire people with a doctorate," he mused. He didn't mention that he himself held half a dozen honorary degrees from Christian colleges and Bible schools.

Several evenings later I parked my car in the huge lot under the Cow Palace and, clutching my Bible, hurried to claim a seat at the crusade press table. Suddenly a horn sounded behind me, and a driver jumped out of his car. "Sir," he said, "Mr. Graham is in the front seat, and he wants you to join him." I went around to the other side as the front door opened.

"Get in, Sherwood," said Billy, moving over. I did, and he introduced me to the others in the car, including his brother Melvin. I didn't know Billy had a brother. As the car moved ahead, Billy patted me on the knee and said, "I want you to know that yours is the finest writing I've ever read about my work."

I was speechless.

"Come and sit with me on the platform," he added.

The rest of the evening was like a dream. I only remember that while sitting next to Billy, I asked him a banal question, "Are you satisfied with the way the crusade has been going?"

He smiled, but his answer was typical. "We are never satisfied, for we are always looking for deeper things."

The next night I was back at the press table.

Sitting at one of those early evening press conferences a few days later, I waited until everyone else had left and then asked, "Mr. Graham, would it be all right if I interviewed some of the people who have made decisions at the crusade and wrote them up?"

"Certainly."

Presto! The man had spoken. Badges were issued. Doors were opened. Introductions were made. Telephones, typewriters, and counselor files became available. Scrapbooks of clippings were brought out. People were tracked down. Publishers became interested. God was smiling.

The crusade ended with a rally in June at Seals Stadium. Nine months later my first book, *Crusade at the Golden Gate,* was released by Harper & Brothers.[4] It contained chapters about San Francisco and its people, Billy and his team, his message—its effectiveness and its outreach. The book also had ten stories about "inquirers" who had found a new relationship with Jesus Christ at the Cow Palace.

June 1, 1972

Dear Mr. Graham

I am seven years old.
I invited Jesus into
my hrat tonight.
I feel happy

Brian Roth

Six

WHY ME?

~

AND THE LORD SAID TO HIM,
"SURELY I WILL BE WITH YOU."

—JUDGES 6:16

The telephone rang late at night on December 18, 1958, at the Hillside Church manse in east Oakland. Sleepily I picked up the receiver, wondering if another drunk was honoring us by choosing our number from the local telephone directory.

"Sherwood?"

"Yes."

"This is Billy Graham."

I threw off the blankets, tipped over the water glass, and sat bolt upright on the edge of the bed.

"Yes, sir."

"I apologize for calling you so late."

"No trouble."

"How are you? And how is Winnie?"

"Both doing great."

"Sherwood, I'm thinking of starting a new paper dealing with evangelism, and I want to know if you would consider becoming the editor."

The discussion that followed was impeded by my accelerated heartbeat. I managed to promise to pray about it and sleep on it and call back the next day.

Sleep? A likely prospect.

At first I looked back. For twenty-five years I had been trying to open publishers' doors that were stuck fast. In that time I had written four lengthy manuscripts, including a doctoral thesis; they all remain in my file drawer. But just in recent days I had been informed from New York that Harper & Brothers had purchased my first honest-to-goodness book, *Crusade at the Golden Gate.*

Then I wondered what this would mean to me, to my future, my family, and my church. And finally my thoughts reverted from the effect to the cause. What kind of person was this? Billy said he had read my writing. So had others, but they never bothered to tell me so. What had he seen in my writing that no one else had?

Then I began to pray, and as I prayed, the question took a different form. What had God put into Billy Graham that enabled him to discern my ability to help him? He had good writers on his staff. In addition, a hundred editors of evangelical Christian publications were available to him if he wanted one of them. In some ways all were better qualified professionally than I, and they had experience galore. How did he know I had what he wanted?

While it was true that I loved the Lord and had years of journalistic training and a classical background in English literature, I was not aware that he knew of that. In fact, I could make out no human explanation.

But, then, could I do the job? The only answer to my prayer that made sense were the words, "Go for it!" God being my helper, I felt in my heart I could carry the message to Garcia, even if no one other than Billy and I believed I could. Just turn me loose.

A pang entered my thoughts about our church. The Oakland congregation we now served was made of such warmhearted people, and I loved (and still love) every one of them. They had changed my views about ecclesiastical inertia. They had responded to my passion for evangelism, had supported the crusade in the Cow Palace, had taken counseling instruction, and had sung in the choir. The membership was increasing, and we were supporting missionaries. Christ's Gospel was bearing fruit. Moreover, we were having fun. Did I really want to leave these people and go back behind a typewriter?

Next day, after praying with my wife (who was pretty excited), I telephoned Billy and accepted. He told me he would keep me advised.

Three months later Billy was preaching the Gospel to the greatest crowds yet of his career in Melbourne, Australia. To us back home the news was breathtaking. It almost sounded as if revival had come at last and the Lord was about to return. On one Sunday afternoon in March, 70,000 people flocked to the Myer Music Bowl to hear the message of salvation. Since the bowl seated 3,000, the rest of the crowd decamped on the sloping grass of the "King's Domain" with their bikes and babies.

I had already submitted my resignation as pastor of Hillside Church when a cablegram came from team member Grady Wilson in Australia instructing me to "come immediately." It seemed Billy wished me to become acquainted with the rest of the team and to write about the astonishing things God was bringing to pass "down under." On March 11, 1959, a number of our church folk crossed the Bay to wish me bon voyage as I boarded a Pan-American prop plane at San Francisco airport, headed for Honolulu, Fiji, and eventually Australia. The next day, my birthday, was swallowed up by the International Dateline.

New friends guided me through the change of planes in Sydney, and four hours later we arrived in Melbourne. The next day was Saturday, and as the Melbourne crusade was coming to a close, I was invited to a huge crusade breakfast honoring the sponsoring committee. In between speeches Billy introduced me as a team member just arrived, who had left "a great church in California." Great church? Well, if not in numbers, it was great in every other way.

All the men on the Graham crusade team welcomed me warmly, yet I couldn't help feeling as if I were in a fiction role out of *Monsieur Beaucaire* or *The Prisoner of Zenda*. These people I was joining had been world famous for ten years. Billy Graham, Cliff Barrows, George Beverly Shea, Tedd Smith, Grady Wilson, Leighton Ford, Joe Blinco—they were household names in millions of Christian homes. They had ministered on every continent. Exposure through television, radio, motion pictures, and crusades had made them the most popular Christian band of men in the world.

Now this new person had joined them. Who's he? Where's he from? Dallas? What? Oakland? How come he's with them? What does he do? Sing?

On Saturday afternoon Jerry Beavan, Billy's tour manager and close assistant, called me to Billy's room. Billy was most cordial and told me he thought it would be good if I "took some meetings."

"What kind of meetings?" I asked in my ignorance.

"Why, go out and preach in churches. We've had any number of requests. Talk to Jerry; he'll arrange it all."

Then I raised a delicate question. The word had spread that the team was leaving Monday afternoon on a flight to the island state of Tasmania to hold rallies. With trepidation I mentioned it to Billy. "Yes, we're going," he said.

"Am I included?"

"I'm afraid not. You see, we're having to double up at the places where we're staying, they're so cramped for space."

"So what do I do?"

"Stay here in the Victoria Hotel. We'll just be away two nights."

Next day was Sunday, and the crowd that gathered for the closing meeting at the Melbourne Cricket Ground was unbelievable. It was the largest in the history of Australia, but in a few weeks it would be surpassed by the numbers in Sydney. Every seat was taken, including the standing room and the royal boxes. By the time I arrived, they had opened up the sacred turf of the playing field. Official attendance was given out as 143,000.[1]

The preparations for the closing meeting were fantastic. Queen Elizabeth II had sent her personal representative. The governor of Victoria read the Bible. President Eisenhower sent greetings. Someone in authority ordered noisy trains alongside the Cricket Ground slowed to a crawl. As in San Francisco the previous year, people around the world had been praying for Melbourne. Our team had been praying too, and God had heard and answered.

Billy Graham chose that afternoon to take on the most formidable political and military enemy of the twentieth century. "The Communists have boasted that they will conquer the whole world," he declared, his sharp words cutting through the air like knives. He pointed his finger for emphasis. *"They will not!"*

Looking back today, I recognize Billy's statement as a true word of prophecy from the Lord. History has vindicated it. But who at the time could have foreseen such a collapse as we have witnessed? In 1959 the Communists already held two-fifths of the planet in thrall. Moscow controlled Central and Eastern Europe. Indochina, Guatemala, North Korea, and all of Africa from Cairo to Capetown were threatened. The Soviets had the H-bomb.

And there was Billy, the dairyman's son from Charlotte, standing straight and tall with arms gesturing and blond hair waving as he predicted with startling clarity the end of the red menace. He looked so strong and yet so frail, one man gripping the attention of the vast throng. But he had not come to talk about communism. He had come to proclaim the truth as it is in Jesus.

When the invitation was given, the entire grassy playing field was filled with inquirers after that truth. It was truly an awesome sight, the first of many in Australia.

By Monday morning I had decided nobody was going to keep me from Tasmania. I paid a visit to the Salvation Army's territorial commissioner in downtown Melbourne and showed him a letter of introduction from a retired Army commissioner friend in Oakland. I asked if there was a cot in the Hobart citadel where I might sleep that night and also the following night in Launceston. He picked up the telephone and called Tasmania. The Hobart commissioner promptly invited me to be a guest in his home, and the commissioner in Launceston followed suit.

Was I nervous about going against orders? What do you think? I was brand-new on the team. Yet when I put the matter in historical perspective, I sensed that even though my chief was telling me one thing, God was telling me another. Billy Graham did not yet have a magazine, but he had an editor. In years to come that editor should possess the benefit of having seen and known what happened to Billy in Tasmania. Suppose something untoward took place? I still had the reporter's instinct: Get the story!

I went to the airline booking office in Melbourne and boldly signed on the team's open travel roster, after which friends rushed me out to the airport. The airplane's twin props were already whirring when we arrived. Billy was standing at the foot of the portable ramp saying goodbye to a committeeman.

As I hurried up, Billy turned to me with a surprised look on his face. I told him I had found a pad for myself in Tasmania and "couldn't stay away." Since it was "all aboard," there was no time to say more.

What do you suppose Billy did? He smiled, put his arm around me, gave me a squeeze, and said, "Bless your heart."

I believe he was listening to the same God who was talking to me. Greatness.

A huge outpouring of Tasmanians greeted the team in Hobart. Next day we made a caravan by auto across Tasmania to Launceston for the second rally. On the route Billy and I spent two hours together in a small car discussing the new magazine.

Two weeks later I accompanied team member Roy Gustafson, Wheaton College President Raymond Edman, and Billy on a plane from Sydney to Auckland, New Zealand, where the rest of the team had already been ministering. A giant reception that included Christian Maori dancers welcomed us in a soccer bowl at Mount Roskill.

First, however, we newcomers were ushered into a private room where members of the crusade committee, the local mayor, and other dignitaries welcomed us. When the formalities ended, it was announced that "the ladies wish to be presented." In trooped a smiling delegation of wives, all properly dressed and wearing hats. Each lady greeted Billy with a handshake and a bow until one buxom Kiwi sister stopped the line. "I am a Maori," she said, "and we don't do it that way."

"How do you do it?" asked Billy.

"We touch noses."

"Well, why not?" Billy obligingly extended his proboscis for the greeting, and everybody laughed.

For the next week I was assigned to be Billy's secretary. His overseas mail was kept in Sydney, but all mail with a New Zealand postmark went through my hands. What a treat! It was my privilege to read private letter after letter written by New Zealand Christians, telling Billy of their love for Jesus. They had found their faith renewed at the crusade meetings and were full of appreciation for his coming to their island country. It was a joy to respond, to thank God for their letters, and to leave them a verse of Scripture and a thought. What dear folks! After all these years my eyes get moist thinking about them and hoping that when we all get to heaven, we shall finally meet.

In eight days one-quarter of the population of New Zealand, half a million people, visited the crusades in the three cities of Auckland, Wellington, and Christchurch.[2] Grady Wilson, Leighton Ford, and Joe Blinco were the advance preachers. We then left on Sunday night and flew to Sydney for the mammoth four-week crusade about to open there. So on to Brisbane, Adelaide, and Perth.

Such an outpouring of spiritual enthusiasm in the continent of Australia has never been equaled before or since. Altogether between January and May 1959, the Graham team held 114 meetings in Australia and New Zealand, which were attended by 3,362,240 persons. Out of this number, 145,041 individuals responded to invitations to receive Christ or rededicate their lives to Him.

One final memory of New Zealand lingers with me. As our plane stood ready to depart Christchurch airport for Sydney with the whole team aboard, a telegram was delivered and handed from row to row and seat to seat for us to read. It was signed by the Christchurch crusade executive committee, and it read: "Go your way, eat the fat, and drink the sweet, and send portions unto them for whom nothing is prepared: for this day is holy unto our Lord: neither be ye sorry; for the joy of the Lord is your strength" (Nehemiah 8:10 KJV).

The joy of the Lord! It carried us across the Tasman Sea and is still with us.

Surrey, B.C.
Jan 5
Dear Billy Graham
I like your
t.v. crusades
I am seven years
old
I think Jesus is
speshel
I love Jesus
I like you
#one way
Lynn Swetnam

Seven

JUST DO IT!

~

I WILL PRAISE YOUR NAME,
FOR YOU HAVE DONE WONDERFUL THINGS.

—ISAIAH 25:1

It was one of the more memorable evenings of my life. Standing near the top of the Sydney Showground, I looked down upon 60,000 people gathered to hear the Gospel of Jesus Christ.

But tonight there was something special. Two thousand nurses, drawn from every hospital in the environs of Sydney, were making their way into the center of the arena. Each wore a colorful cape representing her training institution. When they all rose quietly to be recognized at Cliff Barrows's request, they made a splash of brilliance in the Showground that brought Australians to their feet cheering.

I stood amazed at what I saw. These young women were not on official duty. They were not on parade. Neither were they attracted by royalty or patriotism or professional leadership. No outward lure or compulsion had brought them to the Showground. Instead, something deep inside them had responded to the drawing of the Spirit of God to hear the unspeakable riches of Christ proclaimed by a forty-year-old Baptist minister from North Carolina.

When the invitation came urging people to give their hearts and lives to the Savior, it was thrilling to see scores of colorfully caped inquirers blending in with the thousands who came to the altar. I thought to myself, *This is like heaven—joy and music.* The choir was singing softly, but where I stood under the open sky, I was listening for another choir, rendering the sounds of a heavenly symphony. Can you believe that? Pythagoras, the Greek philosopher, said 2,500 years ago that the stars in their orbits emit harmonious music.

At the close of the meeting, I returned to the platform. As Billy Graham stepped down, he told me to see him before I left for Honolulu and home the next day.

Our meeting took place very early the following morning. Grady Wilson escorted me into Billy's hotel bedroom and then withdrew. Billy was still in bed, sitting up, hair tousled and a smile on his face. He gave me the word—I would be moving to Minneapolis where the managing editor of the new magazine would be my close associate. This man was George M. Wilson (no relation to Grady). He was Billy's business manager, director of his main offices in Minneapolis, and secretary and treasurer of his board of trustees.

Billy thanked me for coming to Australia and said he would be writing me with some fresh ideas regarding the magazine. I thanked him in return, but I had been so moved the night before that the words did not come easily. Finally I said, "Could we have a prayer before I go?"

"Certainly." Billy jumped out of bed in his pajamas and knelt beside it, and I knelt alongside him. After all these years, don't expect me to tell you exactly what we prayed. But I remember something unique about that prayer. There was a special note of joy in it.

Let me digress a minute on that subject. Millions of books have been written on prayer, and some of them are very good. But many people, as every minister knows, have a hard time trying to pray to God. As children they may have had no problem, but as adults they often feel that there is "nothing out there," and they "can't get past the ceiling." Even people at the point of suicide admit to trying prayer and finding "it doesn't work."

When I was younger, even after I entered the ministry, so often my prayers for myself were plagued with guilt and sounded as if I had been chewing on cardboard. They either annoyed me to distraction or bored me to death. I could hear Satan whispering, "Is this an act?

Whom are you kidding?" What C. S. Lewis called "the real I" was smothered by my self-consciousness.

When I finally learned from some godly men how to pray for others, the Holy Spirit put wings to my words. I became an intercessor and began to have fun. I was caught up in the magnificent realization of how good and how great God is. Talk about fellowship! Prayer became a time of joy and praise.

I learned that once we stop asking for something and start giving thanks to God instead, the whole nature of prayer changes. Instead of tedium, there is sparkle. I learned too that the reason God wants us to glorify Him is so we will stop glorifying ourselves.

Billy and I did not waste time that morning praying for ourselves; we prayed for each other, for our families, and for the people of Australia. What a ball that was! What excitement! What power of intercession! I could have stayed there a long time.

Are you having trouble with your prayer life? Get together with somebody and pour some praise into your prayers. You'll find out, as Augustine did, that the reason God gave us tongues in the first place was so we could pray and talk with Him.[1] If you are tired of mournful, wailing prayers, so is He! If you're cooped up in some kind of solitary retreat like a hermit, He doesn't like that any more than you do. Laugh, sing, shout—even make merry, without any false or artificial stimulus, and God will join you. Make prayer the high point of the day. He'll love it.

After Billy and I spent a few minutes on our knees together, I rose feeling greatly refreshed. A final word, a handshake, and I was out the door and on my way to the airport and across the Pacific, bursting with anticipation at what the Lord was about to do.

In due time a lengthy letter arrived from Billy. It was all about the new magazine. He said he was convinced that profound truths could be expressed in simple language. He wanted the magazine to be relevant, thought-provoking, timely, spiritual, devotional, yet with a breezy, easy-to-read style.

After several more paragraphs of detailed instruction, Billy concluded, "This is quite a big order; however, I believe it can be done and will meet a real need. I believe the Lord has led you to this important ministry and am thankful for your willingness to obey His voice in this matter. With warmest personal greetings, Billy Graham."

This letter brought me back to earth. The words "big order . . . important ministry" required me to face certain facts. That I could write I knew—but to edit a magazine? In my heart of hearts I confessed I had not the slightest idea how to do it.

Newspapers were a piece of cake. I had worked on four of them in California, Hawaii, and Alaska. I knew page layouts, dummies, linotype machines, and flatbed presses. But artwork? Photojournalism? Lithographic plates? Halftones, duotones, silverprints, color keys? They were words that had not yet entered my vocabulary.

A week later, when on an errand in San Francisco, I paid a visit to the offices of *Sunset* magazine. With some embarrassment I asked a girl in the business office, "Can anybody here give me some information on putting out a magazine? I mean, what do you do?" The people to whom I was referred were kind and pleasant but busy. No one could help me. *Sunset*, they pointed out, was not a religious magazine. A summary of their advice was "just do it!"

Since the magazine would be published in Minneapolis, Minnesota, the international headquarters of the Billy Graham Evangelistic Association, I arranged for our family to move east. We drove into Minneapolis on July 1, 1959. The following Monday I was given an office in the BGEA and went to work.

The first thing I discovered was that the staff people who work for Billy Graham are of very special quality. They welcomed my family with a genuine warmth that reflected the love of Christ. In fact, they did not (and still do not) consider themselves as working for an individual person at all, but rather for the Savior of mankind, the Lord Jesus Christ.

I learned that while they attend a wide variety of churches, they are single-minded when it comes to the cause of evangelism. As personnel in a business office, their main function is receiving and answering mail, which they do with great efficiency. On the personal side, they neither smoke nor swear. They do not tell off-color stories or engage in office politics or pad their expense books or complain or strike or harass. They are honest with God's money. They pray a lot, and they also smile a lot. In fact, they are God's unique, beautiful servants, and in the seventeen years I spent in their midst, they had a salutary effect on me. I counted it a singular privilege to labor alongside them.

Now that my feet were planted in the upper Midwest, I was forced to bite the bullet, and vocational shock set in. No longer was I a pastor with a Sunday sermon to prepare. I had become an organization man, and the time had passed when I could put off the dismal truth: As a magazine editor, I was a failure before I even started. I didn't know how to "just do it."

Billy had sent me copies of British Christian magazines, and American periodicals were available in the Billy Graham headquarters. I spent hours and days thumbing through them and became increasingly perturbed. It was evident that the message of salvation, the message Billy preached, was not "hot copy." The magazines were without exception topical. Denominational subjects were of primary interest. As a newspaperman, I had spent many of my working hours reporting local news of people going here and there and doing this and that. Scanning the religious magazines, I realized that they were publishing the same kind of thing, the only difference being that the people they wrote about were in some way "religious."

This was intolerable. Billy Graham wanted a magazine that would bring Christ to the nations. He wanted to take on the Devil himself. He wanted to shake up the church and put it on the front lines. While we were in Australia, Dr. Raymond Edman, then president of Wheaton College, told me that back in 1949 and 1950 when Billy and Cliff and their teammates first saw the amazing response to their meetings *everywhere they went*, they actually came to believe God was going to change the human race and bring the world to Christ!

And here I was to be their editor.

"God," I prayed, "what have I gotten into? Billy doesn't want me to publish his message; he wants me to publish Your message. He wants to proclaim Jesus Christ to everybody everywhere, and that's what I want. How in heaven's name can I do it?"

Gradually I began to assemble some preliminary thoughts as to what such a magazine should say. It should glorify God and nobody else. It should talk about basic things and avoid pushing some pet position or other. It should be interesting, even fascinating, with exciting stories about God and people. It should reflect the Holy Spirit and also the spirit of Billy and the team. It should make people laugh and cry just as Jesus did. It should leap over every barrier that Christians set up against each other. It should love everybody and discriminate against nobody. It should underscore the trustworthiness of the Bible. It should hate sin but love the sinner. It should bring people to the Cross. It should be upbeat and cheerful, knowing that Jesus is coming soon for His own.

I took a large sheet of paper and began to make a dummy of what I thought the front page of the first issue of the magazine should look like. Then the buzzer sounded. In the churches I served there were no buzzers, but the Billy Graham Evangelistic Association is no church. So this new organization man sighed, rose up, put on a smile, and dutifully went to the cafeteria for coffee.

Eight

DAKOTA DETOUR

~

BLESSED ARE THE PEOPLE WHO KNOW THE JOYFUL SOUND! . . .
FOR YOU ARE THE GLORY OF THEIR STRENGTH.

—PSALM 89:15, 17

Returning to my desk, I looked over what the day's labors had accomplished. To my dismay—make that horror—I found that I had duplicated the same kind of patchwork dummy I used to make when I was city editor of the six-page *Alaska Daily Press* in Juneau (pop. 6,000) twenty years earlier. The press run of this new magazine of Billy's was expected to reach hundreds of thousands of readers, if not millions, on all six continents. The press run of our little Alaskan daily was 1,375 copies, and its Juneau "outreach" was one road extending twenty-one miles north and three miles south.[1]

My first layout never made it into the Billy Graham Center archives. It went into the wastebasket before the artist could get a look at it.

One fine day I was invited into the office of the general manager, treasurer, and corporate vice president of the BGEA, George Wilson. "Woody," he said, "you're a great guy, and you've written a terrific book about San Francisco, but this is Minneapolis, and there's nothing here for you to do yet. You can't edit a magazine until there's a magazine, and we can't have a magazine until the mailing list is computerized, and the computers aren't even here yet." He looked at me over his half-glasses. "We're not ready for you."

"But . . . "

He smiled. "We have a film exhibitor going around to churches in South Dakota showing *Mr. Texas* and *Oiltown, U.S.A.*, and he tells me there's a church out there that wants to have you come and preach to them for a week. He told them about you."

"Really? What did he say?" I asked, thinking about my notebooks crammed full of old sermons.

Mr. Wilson ignored my question. "Would you like to do that, or wouldn't you?"

Pressure! No alternatives! "Why not?"

He nodded. "Preach the Word and give an invitation," he said. (Memo to myself: Forget the notebooks.) "Take an expense book and turn in your mileage." Wilson turned back to his desk. I left him thinking to myself, *For this I left a nice portfolio in a sunny California parish with vacations in Yosemite?*

Pollock, South Dakota, was a brand-new town in a rich farming area near the North Dakota border. Completion of the giant Oahe Dam across the Missouri River had caused an exceptionally generous federal government to move the entire community to higher ground, with new housing, street lights, sewers, and even churches, while backed-up dam waters flooded the old town.

The people of the congregation welcomed me with open arms. They genuinely seemed to like me—not that anybody had ever heard of me or read my book. All there was going for me was that I worked for Billy Graham, and that was enough. Everybody in South Dakota loved Billy Graham. Well, almost everybody.

For a week I preached in that church night after night and tried my best to "do the work of an evangelist."[2] The services were well supported and well attended, and the people were appreciative. They couldn't help it if I neither looked nor sounded like Billy Graham. How many of those present were Christians I could not know; but despite all the intercession, the response at the altar was *nada*.

The chief problem was not my lack of understanding of biblical doctrine or poor preparation or the possible resistance of a rustic congregation or the acoustics or the music or anything like that. The problem was my digestive tract. I was so stuffed with healthy, delicious, delectable Dakota cuisine the entire week that I felt like a balloon.

Each day at noon and at six o'clock a farmer would drive up to the church manse where I was staying and take me in his pickup truck to the farmhouse where his beaming housewife would treat me to the most sumptuous meal I had ever eaten. Why? Because I was Billy Graham's friend, that's why. At one farmhouse I counted seventeen dishes being passed around the table. Roast beef, gravy, mashed potatoes, sweet potatoes, peas, green beans, celery, carrots, corn-on-the-cob, cauliflower, asparagus, squash, parsnips, beets, lemon pie, coffee—you name it. And the risk of offending the housewife was too great—I had to eat and eat.

Let me add that I found the people of South Dakota to be the salt of the earth. They loved God, they loved their church and their country, and, as I said, they loved Billy Graham. Many of them listened on Sunday afternoon to Billy's radio broadcast, *The Hour of Decision*.[3] They peppered me with questions about the man and his team. They wanted to know more about his wife, Ruth, whom I had not met. They were fascinated to hear about the great meetings in Australia that verged on revival. Some of them were already planning to attend the 1960 crusade in Minneapolis.

My host pastor, Reverend Benjamin Cedar, and his saintly wife, Berniece, had been enthusiastic supporters of Billy Graham for years. One of their sons, Paul, whom I met during that week with his young bride, Jeannie, later became a Graham crusade associate. More recently he served a term as president of the Evangelical Free Church of America.

Because of the people's affection for my boss, all the hospitality of South Dakota seemed to be poured out on me. I gave up breakfasts and spent hours shaking down the luncheons and dinners by trudging the prairie roads. Dakota roads run north, south, east, and west. One day I walked clear to North Dakota, but it proved difficult going because every car that passed by tried to give me a lift.

At the closing service on Sunday night a young lady visiting from Aberdeen, a friend of Paul and Jeannie, came forward at the invitation and gave her heart to Jesus Christ. At last, a soul! It was the

Lord's doing, it was beautiful, and I was grateful. My vocation as a crusade evangelist was off the ground—but barely, like the *Spruce Goose*.

Later a church in Stickney, South Dakota, beckoned me for another week of meetings. Again I enjoyed the fellowship and the high privilege of preaching the Gospel of Jesus Christ, but my memory fades as to the response to my closing invitations. The people were most gracious and assured me of their love for Billy Graham. They fed me magnificently and then took me pheasant hunting. In turn I promised every family in the entire congregation a year's free subscription to Billy's magazine when and if it appeared.

Before invitations to preach came flooding in to me from all over the upper Midwest, my evangelistic ministry abruptly collapsed. I was whisked back to the Minneapolis headquarters to my family and a leaner diet.

One more thing should be said about those visits to South Dakota. They convinced me that the reception the people gave me was symptomatic of the way people felt—and still feel—about Billy Graham all over North America. I could have gone to forty-nine other states and been welcomed the same way. George Wilson was speaking the truth in 1960 when he told me that Billy Graham received mail from every post office in the United States. My aim in writing this book, apart from the sheer joy of it, is to try to explain why.

Winola and I had decided to enroll our son Alexander in the Stony Brook School on Long Island for one year. That accomplished, we were assigned to take part in the Billy Graham crusades in Wheaton, Illinois, and Indianapolis, Indiana.

At Wheaton my duties were limited to team activities, serving as counselor to inquirers at the meetings and lecturing in English classes at Wheaton College. On the college campus Winola and I had the thrill of meeting Ruth Bell Graham, Billy's wife, about whom we had heard so much. She herself is an honored alumna of the college, and she spoke briefly at a rally for coed students in the school gymnasium.

After Ruth finished counseling with an inquirer, we introduced ourselves and were utterly charmed by her. Here was a lady of poise and distinction with a disarming smile and great literary accomplishments. We became firm friends. Not long afterward we were guests in their North Carolina home.

In October I joined some Minneapolis staff members in traveling to Indianapolis, where we became part of a crusade that was warmly received by that capital city. I made it my business to master the inside operation of a Billy Graham crusade. To that end I visited executive committee meetings, counselor training classes (later called Christian Life and Witness classes), choir rehearsals, and usher briefing sessions. My shoe-leather investigation covered local church relations, special arrangements for open local prayer, visitation evangelism training, television evangelism sessions, follow-up, colaborers' corps, designation committee meetings, children's ministry, security, the audio system, parking arrangements, first aid, and press relations. I visited them all.

Almost the entire working party of this huge endeavor, I discovered, was made up of volunteers, hundreds of them, all eager to serve the Lord in a wide spectrum of capacities.

Indianapolis was a successful crusade from start to finish because at the heart and soul of the Hoosier people is a firm belief in God, a belief that the acids of modernity have yet to corrode. One memorable crusade evening saw the front rows filled with uniformed Indiana state troopers as special guests. A stirring moment occurred when Cliff Barrows invited them all to cluster around Billy Graham on the platform, and the vast audience stood and joined in singing "Onward Christian Soldiers."

Two other incidents at the Indianapolis crusade of 1959 have stayed with me. On a Sunday afternoon in October I rode back from the racetrack to our hotel in a car with Billy Graham in the front seat. On the way he turned around and said to me, "My wife fell in love with your wife." Those words sent sweet music into my soul.

The other incident took place at an informal party of team members and volunteer workers at the close of the crusade. Billy Zeoli, now president of a Christian motion picture company in Muskegon, Michigan, was at that time director of Indianapolis Youth for Christ and was active on the crusade committee. Tall, dark, and talented, he had managed to get hold of a blond wig and was wondering whether he dared repeat his popular imitation of Dr. Graham preaching in the presence of the man himself.

After consulting others about it, Billy Zeoli finally went to Dr. Graham personally for approval. That gentleman's reaction was, "Billy, you go ahead and do it, and I'll be the first to laugh!" The performance was a roaring success.

Nine

IKE'S PUTTING GREEN

～

SO DAVID WENT ON . . .
AND THE LORD GOD OF HOSTS WAS WITH HIM.

—2 SAMUEL 5:10

O ur plane approached National Airport, and we saw the panorama of Washington, D.C., beneath us in all its white splendor. While we soared over the monuments, domes, and spires, once again I felt those old red, white, and blue chills running up and down my spine.

I've always been a lover of America. As a first grader, I would stand up and say with my classmates, "I pledge allegiance to *my flag* . . ." When Pearl Harbor was bombed in 1941, I couldn't wait to get into uniform. Even today, as an octogenarian in the 1990s, when I hear John Philip Sousa's "Stars and Stripes Forever," I want to start marching around the living room.

Greatness is to be found in Washington, D.C., if one knows where to look—in the past. It can be studied at the Capitol, the Lincoln Memorial, the National Archives, the Smithsonian Institution. I felt it while climbing the 555 steps inside the Washington Monument. Surely God had a role in choosing the superb leadership that brought our nation into existence and gave us our Constitution. Probably the finest thing Ronald Reagan did during his presidency was to bring back some of that eighteenth-century feeling of pride in America and America's greatness.

When my family and I moved to Washington, D.C., in 1960, the scene sizzled with political heat. President Eisenhower, now finishing his second term, faced a sudden crisis as Marxist-Leninist communism spread within ninety miles of the United States. Fidel Castro had announced Cuba's alliance with the Soviet Union. Meanwhile Khrushchev shot down our U-2 spy plane over Moscow and was rattling his H-Bomb with one hand while banging his shoe on the table in the United Nations Assembly with the other. China and Lebanon were threatening the peace, and the Simbas were murdering American missionaries in the Congo. From the Senate and House galleries we watched the jockeying as future candidates John Kennedy and Richard Nixon and their partisans struggled for preference and power.

I came to the city on temporary assignment to serve as an editorial assistant to Dr. Carl F. H. Henry, renowned editor of *Christianity Today*. This magazine inspired by Billy Graham four years earlier had now become the most influential periodical of evangelical Christianity in America, thanks to the brilliant leadership of Editor Henry and Executive Editor L. Nelson Bell. I wrote editorials, reviewed books, covered religious events, and sat in staff conferences with the two editors, who became my beloved friends. My time on the "*C.T.*" staff gave me valuable experience in magazine production. I no longer felt like an ignoramus about such things as graphics and offset printing.

From the window of my office on the tenth floor of the Washington building, I looked down directly on the White House half a block away. I noticed outside the presidential mansion a tiny patch of green grass with a flag on a stick. That, I was advised, was President Eisenhower's private putting green. *Aha!* I thought. *Ike, I've got you covered.* When I wasn't writing sharply critical editorials about the liberals and radicals in the mainline church leadership, I kept my eye on that green patch.

Ike, however, had his hands full with Comrade Castro. His unused putting green became a symbol of my own dissatisfaction. For over a year I had been filling in here and there while waiting to go to work for Billy. The world in 1960 was such a mess, and the only solution I could see was Jesus Christ. My heart was in the Midwest where a new magazine was about to appear, designed to bring millions of readers to faith in God and salvation in His Son, Jesus Christ. The appeal to this journalist-in-waiting was irresistible.

Carl Henry and Nelson Bell urged me to stay in Washington and become one of *Christianity Today*'s editors. But what could I do about the world situation? Or the church situation, for that matter? I agreed with Lord Acton that "power tends to corrupt, and absolute power corrupts absolutely."[1] I just wanted to go to Minneapolis and start writing for Jesus and winning souls for His kingdom. At the moment what I seemed to be doing was like practicing on Ike's putting green, tapping little white balls into a cup.

In June 1960, much to our family's delight, the Billy Graham team arrived in Washington for a one-week crusade. Sensitive to the predicament the world was in, Billy had acceded to the urging of Christian leaders in government and had agreed to come to the national capital and point the nation to Christ. Billy felt, and still feels, about America the way I do.

While the crusade was in progress, I was invited to a team meeting in a hotel where I renewed my friendship with this wonderful band of men. It felt so good to be back with them. As we spent a little time together, I made an interesting observation. As long as Billy was out of the room, the team was relaxed. They were a grand bunch of fellows, full of light banter and even hilarity. Grady Wilson was at his best with his unique and devastating brand of humor. Then Billy entered, and things changed. It wasn't that he cast a pall; it was just that we all suddenly sensed a call to responsibility. A different ambience pervaded the room. Now we were thoughtful, serious, even devout, ready and eager to apply ourselves to a world of need and God's business at hand—until Billy himself began to smile.

As we sat around the long table, Billy called on me for an account of my stewardship in Washington. I spoke briefly about my work at *C.T.* and mentioned a visit to the Holy Land with Dr. Henry. Then I confessed, "I've been here nearly six months and have been invited to preach just twice. Finally I went to a Salvation Army rally and stood up without being asked and gave my testimony just to hear how it sounded." That evoked a laugh, and Grady Wilson said, "Thank God for the Army!"

The closing service of the Greater Washington Crusade was held outdoors on Sunday afternoon in Griffith Stadium, once home to the Washington Senators baseball club. My wife, our thirteen-year-old son Alexander, and I had passes that allowed us to sit in the reserved section of the bleachers. Shortly after the meeting began with Cliff Barrows leading the audience in singing "How Great Thou Art," two large gentlemen seated themselves in the row just behind us.

I recognized one of them as "LBJ," Senator Lyndon Baines Johnson of Texas. This future president of the United States would later become a particular friend to Billy and Ruth Graham. Turning around after the song, I introduced myself and my family and shook hands with the senator, telling him we felt honored to be in his presence. He in turn introduced us to his companion, Senator George Smathers of Florida.

Our son Alex was sitting directly in front of the senators and overheard their conversation. He told us later that the two men spent the entire afternoon engaged in political discussion, except for one brief interlude. It was during Billy's closing invitation asking people to come forward in commitment to Jesus Christ as Savior and Master and Lord. At that point Johnson turned to his companion and asked, "What are all those people doing going out there on the field?"

Senator Smathers's reply, as reported by our son, was, "Oh, they're just making a promise to go to church!"

In mid-July Billy Graham wrote me from Montreux, Switzerland, "If at all possible, it is my desire that you attend our conference here in Montreux beginning August 16 for three days. We have about thirty-five personal friends and colaborers coming to meet with us. This will enable you to meet men from other parts of the world who are of like mind."

On the first day of the Montreux gathering in August 1960, an attempt was made to substitute another agenda for the one Billy and his colleagues had planned. I was much impressed by the quiet way in which Billy, with eloquent assistance from Stephen Olford, got the program back on track without any unusual distraction. He showed the same diplomatic skill he had exercised in the London pub with Cassandra.

Searching discussions followed for three days on such topics as "The Attestations of the Holy Spirit Today," "Church-State Relationships Throughout the World," "Communicating the Gospel to Underprivileged Peoples," and "Repentance, Rejoicing, and Revival."

That gathering on the shore of Lake Geneva became the prototype of the epochal evangelistic congresses that Billy Graham initiated and conducted in Berlin (1966), Lausanne, Switzerland (1974), and Amsterdam (1983 and 1986). Tens of thousands of Christian evangelists from all over the world gained recognition and inspiration at those unparalleled events. If they did nothing else, the congresses established Billy Graham as the premier Christian evangelist of the twentieth century.

It was at this conference I came to understand why Billy Graham's crusades, while not free from quiet emotion such as tears, are divinely protected from ostentatious behavior everywhere he goes. Many have recognized that Billy's ministry of evangelism avoids incurring the manifestations of extreme behavior that have hurt the ministries of revivalists of the past and laid them open to severe criticism. In that connection an outstanding American church historian, Professor Sydney A. Ahlstrom of Yale University, published an article in 1960 that mentioned Billy. He wrote, "A brief consideration of Billy Graham is in order, for upon his manly shoulders has rested the burden of reviving mass evangelism and preventing it from becoming only a cheap and emotional accommodation of vague American yearnings or a sentimental reversion to a not-so-old 'old-time religion.' Not significantly realized, however, is his solitariness in the field."[2]

To me it is wonderfully heartwarming to have a godly educator such as Professor Ahlstrom (called by *Time* magazine "America's premier church historian") recognize that God was using a man of average academic attainments to achieve His divine purpose for the conduct of worship. And Billy was doing it with distinction.

After three days the meetings devoted to evangelism adjourned, and two days later a special meeting of the Graham team was convened. During it Billy pointed his finger at me. "Woody," he announced, "we are ready to start the magazine. Go back to Minneapolis as fast as you can and get out the first issue."

Cheers! Goodbye, putting green. After a year and a half, the hour had struck. As soon as the meeting ended, I packed my suitcase and walked to the depot to catch the Swiss electric train bound for Geneva. Nor did I stop traveling until my plane landed at Twin Cities International Airport, where my family was happily waiting for me.

THE
LEAF
BLADE

~

August 1st 1971

Dear Billy Graham,

My name is Mark Patton and I am ten years old. I have donated a dollar and I would like some <u>stickers</u>. Last night I have just come to one of your Crusades. It was the best show I have ever been to. Before this my sister and I would fight every day. Now that I and her have given our lives to God, we are laughing together, playing together having fun together, doing everything together. I thank you for your crusades and everybody else that helped. I am a much happier person now.

Love, Mark Patton

P.S. Heres a sdf addressed envelope.

Ten

THE FIRST ISSUE

~

THE WORDS OF THE WISE ARE LIKE GOADS,
AND THE WORDS OF SCHOLARS ARE LIKE WELL-DRIVEN NAILS,
GIVEN BY ONE SHEPHERD.

—ECCLESIASTES 12:11

During my time in the East that spring I had visited the office of *Christian Herald* magazine and also the Manhattan offices of the Associated Press and United Press International, where I talked with their religion writers. I found that the wire services, generally so impartial toward public figures, were strangely and curiously drawn to the person of Billy Graham. Why was that? Was Billy an attractive kind of surrogate for God to some of these amiable unchurched people, a reminder that they too must die and face the judgment? I don't know; but as for advice about my new job, I got nothing.

My last stop in New York City was at 405 West 23rd Street, the editorial office of the *Watchman-Examiner*, a venerable American Baptist publication, now expired. I enjoyed reading the thoughtful editorials in this magazine. They *said* something. After climbing several flights of wooden stairs, I knocked at the door and was admitted by the longtime editor, Rev. John Bradbury.

This odd little man with bushy, sandy-colored hair (I'm not sure it was his) pursed his lips and spoke in a high-pitched voice as he invited me to sit down. He then seated himself before a rolltop desk in his high-ceilinged office. As he leaned back in his swivel chair with his feet dangling, it was for me a moment frozen in time. I felt the way Conway had in James Hilton's *Lost Horizon* when he entered Shangri-la and was taken to see the 200-year-old Luxembourg missionary, Perrault.[1]

In a few words I told him of the assignment given to me and said that I was seeking advice from experienced editors. These were the days before audio tapes, and as Bradbury began to speak, I reached for my note pad.

"Mr. Wirt," he said, "there is a hiatus in the magazine publishing business. There used to be Christian publications that lifted up the Lord and carried a theme of devotion, that talked about Jesus Christ and emphasized His work and the Holy Spirit, that explained what it means to walk with God. Our magazines don't do that any more, and it's a pity."

Those words were a talisman to my soul. I thought, *By the grace of God, that's the kind of magazine I want to see us publish*. I had found what I was looking for.

A month later on the flight from Geneva to Minneapolis to carry out Billy's instructions, I finally got down to some intensive praying and note-making. From the perspective of church history, what would this magazine be like? From the perspective of journalism, what would shape its unique character? All our months of preparation had reached the moment of launching. But launching what? A tub, like the one the early film comedian Buster Keaton built, that made a nice splash in the water and then sank right to the bottom? Plenty of new magazines do that.

In September I received a long letter from Billy explaining precisely what he had in mind. It was in effect a confirmation of what I had learned from John Bradbury. In addition to specific details about the first issue, Billy wrote this remarkable statement (which *Decision* would carry on its editorial page):

> It has been evident for some time that there is a need for good devotional and evangelistic literature that could be made available not only to those who have made inquiries and decisions at our crusades, but also to the whole body of the church. The value of literature in winning the minds of the uncommitted is being clearly demonstrated by the

Communists. *Decision* is to be a mass-produced paper translated eventually into many languages, and preparations are now under way for French, German, and Spanish translations to appear early next year.

The purpose of this paper, therefore, is twofold: to provide spiritual food for Christians who normally do not have much Christian literature available to them and to publish evangelistic messages and articles aimed at reaching the secular mind and winning the nonbeliever to Christ. We shall seek to make the paper attractive and easy to read by "putting the cookies on the lower shelf," as D. L. Moody once expressed it. (Moody added, "So the children can get at them.")

While there will be an appeal to the intellectual, it is not primarily for the intellectual that this paper is written. It is designed for the ordinary people who are busily engaged in a secular world where there is tremendous competition for their time. I am convinced that profound truths can be stated in simple terms, and to that end we intend to publish carefully selected materials dealing with the Christian life, drawn from the whole treasury of Scripture and Christian writing.

We shall seek a balanced presentation of the Gospel. Doctrine will be used as the New Testament uses it, to strengthen the life and walk of the Christian.

There are other things we hope the paper will accomplish. We shall endeavor to maintain a link between the team and those whose prayers, deeds, and gifts have been upholding us through the years. We would like to share with you the results of this ministry as the Holy Spirit leads and blesses and to tell you of our hopes and dreams for the future as God wills. We shall have occasional testimonies of lives that have been transformed by the grace of our Lord Jesus Christ.

Decision will also have a distinctive ministry to encourage the hearts of pastors and missionaries everywhere. We intend to carry at least two full-length evangelistic messages each month, together with devotional and sermonic material that can be used by busy pastors who are searching for sermon material. We also intend to keep Christians informed of evangelistic strategy within the life of the church and even to help the church clarify its definition of evangelism. This paper will not emphasize any particular denomination but will be addressed to the church universal.

There will be sections devoted to the discussion of theological, social, and evangelistic issues of our day. Some of the articles will be purposefully controversial. We believe there is room for high-level disagreement and discussion to arouse the church out of indifference and complacency. It is also our prayer that God will see fit to use this paper to fan the flames of spiritual awakening in many parts of the world.

We know that many of our friends will have questions to ask after reading this first issue. They will wonder why no mention was made of some particular aspect of Christian truth. Do these pages really make a full-orbed presentation of the Christian faith? Others will have questions to raise regarding policies of publication and distribution.

To all of you we send Paul's reminder that patience works experience, and experience hope. This issue is the result of months of prayer and labor on the part of many, but it is far from being complete in itself. The Gospel is manifold, as future issues will illustrate.

Meanwhile we cherish your encouragement and spiritual support. The financial cost of this publication is tremendous—far beyond our present capacities. However, we have taken it as a step of faith. We believe the world situation is getting more desperate with every passing hour. Something must be done on a mass scale, quickly and effectively. We believe as *Decision* is scattered in many languages throughout the world, seed will be sown that will eventually bring great spiritual results.[2] We need your help if the venture is to succeed.

I trust you will sustain our editorial and publication staff with your prayers. This is an awesome undertaking in many ways. We tremble to think of this added responsibility. We have been encouraged by our friends and advisers all over the world. This first issue of *Decision* is launched in the midst of a revolutionary world at a time when Christianity is being challenged on a scale unprecedented in its history. We therefore covet your prayers and support as we go forward together "with a view to the fitting of the saints for the work of the ministry, for an upbuilding of the body of Christ, until we all advance in the oneness of the faith and of the full knowledge of the Son of God into a man of full growth, into a measure of stature of the fulness of the Christ."

What an assignment for the one-time city editor of the second leading daily newspaper in Juneau, Alaska! You can be sure I subscribed heartily to every word of it.

While flying back from Switzerland to Minnesota in August 1960, I had done some scribbling of my own about the new magazine. First of all, I wrote, it would be God's magazine. It would be chained to no other pillar than the Gospel of our Lord Jesus Christ.

Second, it would be Billy's magazine, reflecting his love for Jesus, his evangelistic zeal, his commitment to and understanding of the Bible, his personality, mission, ministry, theology, love for people, compassion, vision, and goals.

Third, the magazine would be influenced by and would belong to the millions of prayer partners and admirers of Billy Graham around the world who would subscribe to it, read it, digest it, and pass it on.

Finally, it would be under my stewardship, augmented by the counsel of my superiors and coworkers. Together we would try to please the Father of Lights, the angels, the Graham family (especially Ruth), the BGEA people, the subscribers on the mailing list, the Christian public, the unbelieving public, the postal authorities, seniors, children, and just about everybody this side of the principalities and powers of darkness. Then might our new magazine become an inspiring and transforming vehicle of the Spirit of God to this generation!

Upon reporting for duty at Minneapolis, I was cordially received by George Wilson and escorted to the top floor in the Billy Graham headquarters. There he showed me our huge new computerized machines, the first to be installed in the Twin Cities. These were the "wonders" of the modern world that in 1960 would funnel the message of Christ to every post office in the United States and to readers on every continent.

I was also greeted by the other colleagues who would make up our editorial staff: Dr. Robert O. Ferm, associate editor; Russell Busby, photographer; Robert Blewett, artist; Alice Sundstrom, copy editor; and Martha Warkentin, my new secretary.

Mr. Wilson, with all his other portfolios, would be the managing editor of the magazine and would oversee the whole physical operation. That included bookkeeping, production, paper, ink, printing, mailing, circulation, transport, personnel, equipment, and costs. Everything except editorial content would be under his direct supervision. So if Billy was the magazine's maker, George was its shaper. He even gave the magazine its name, *Decision*.

One of the orders I received from Billy in Australia was "work closely with George." I had already found that this genius George Wilson was a unique individual. Some apparently seemed a bit timid around him. Not so I. I recognized him as my superior and treated him as my friend.

Dr. Robert Ferm was an excellent writer, educator, and Baptist minister who had already published successful books about evangelism and conversions. In Billy's ministry he held many important team portfolios besides being associate editor of the new magazine. Bob Ferm was a popular team member and was noted for his singing in quartets, his flashy sport jackets, and his genial sense of humor. He was a most cooperative editor, and he became a solid friend. Now he is in heaven, and I miss him.

Russ Busby had been Billy's staff photographer since the Oklahoma City crusade of 1956. Among his perennial assets even today are a deep faith, a beautiful wife, and a running line of salty comments on life in general that has kept people laughing down the decades. He is still active, still taking superb pictures, and living in southern California. His favorite text as a photographer, he says, is taken (out of context) from Jeremiah 1:8: "Be not afraid of their faces: for I am with thee to deliver thee, saith the Lord."

Robert Blewett was *Decision*'s art director, an experienced and able painter and illustrator and a highly qualified layout expert. We

The first issue: Associate Editor Robert Ferm (standing) confers with the editor as Decision takes shape. Its circulation eventually reached five million copies in six languages.

were to work together closely for nine years, and the success of the magazine owes much to him. Another staff artist upon whose talents we drew was young Howard Sanden, now known as John Howard Sanden of Carnegie Hall, New York. After leaving BGEA, Sanden achieved wide recognition and is today considered America's premier portraitist. I had to smile when in a recent letter to me, he referred to his years on Billy Graham's staff as "the glory days." Howard's stunning portraits of Mr. and Mrs. Graham are now hung in the lobby of the Billy Graham Training Center at The Cove, founded by the Grahams near Asheville, North Carolina.

Alice Sundstrom—faithful, quiet, and dedicated—was the best copy reader I ever knew. She spared me the indignity of a host of embarrassing typos and other errors.

Billy Graham continued to write me letters after the first issue appeared. He wondered if the magazine shouldn't be expanded to twenty-four pages instead of sixteen. He recommended the style of the Roman Catholic publication, *Our Sunday Visitor*, as being "popular" and "easy-to-read." He urged me to obtain the printed reports of Keswick Week conferences.[3] He wanted the magazine to have a strong missionary emphasis, a sound theology, and a "broad outreach in fellowship."

"These early issues," he wrote, "will be of strategic importance, as they will be analyzed and studied by religious leaders around the world. I hope you will put the best of everything into it." That letter threw a scare into me. The best of what? *Put me under the scrutiny of religious leaders*, I thought, *and see what you get.* And what did he mean by "everything"? If I disappointed him, would he ship me back to California?

One letter from Billy that has meant the most to me came early. It read: "Dear Woody: Just a note to say that I have read through your manuscript for the first issue of Decision. I think it is terrific!" Thank God.

Billy's refusal to exalt himself and his organization has always been one of his most attractive and endearing traits. Surely here are intimations of greatness. To some extent his modesty even rubbed off on me. When I began working for him, I stopped using the letters *Ph.D.* after my name. Considering my position, what was the point? I was helping a man who knew the perfect freedom of Jesus Christ. It was not unreasonable to want a piece of that freedom.

But it did not take me long to decide what should be the magazine's specific content, because the Holy Spirit had already decided it. Of course, it would include a message by Billy Graham in each issue. Where? It didn't matter. As long as I have known him, Billy has never been one to claim the spotlight for himself. His name is often overexposed by publicists but not at his request; quite the contrary. In one of his early letters to me, he wrote, "I insist that my name be taken off the masthead. I must decrease, and He must increase."[4]

Because I knew more women than men would read the magazine, I determined to appeal to men by emphasizing both youth and masculinity—not, however, at the expense of the ladies, without whose company we would be shorn and shriven. People of every race and color and language and every branch of Christendom would find themselves welcome in our pages. Rich people, poor people, old people, men, women, children would all be appealed to. We would search the pages of church history, we would go into the bush hunting for missionaries, we would seek out the great and lowly asking the same question: "Did Jesus die for you? Is He dwelling in you? Tell us about it. Speak up!"

Testimonies? Absolutely, but the emphasis would not be on the Christian enterprise in which the person was engaged. Rather it should be on how Jesus Christ affected his or her life, how the Spirit of God entered the soul and brought about conversion, and how that conversion affected other people.

Because we functioned as the Graham team, not just as individuals, I felt the magazine should highlight the work of different team members. Also, knowing the clergy, I felt the magazine should carry sermon outlines, choice illustrations, and one-liners for hard-pressed ministers. Due to our large Canadian circulation (200,000), I decided we would try to feature Canadians regularly.

Finally, I was determined that the magazine be something other than a solemn religious periodical. The presence of the Lord should give it a bright glow, a flair, a cheerful tone that would imbue issue after issue. Instead of interminable threats, warnings, and forebodings, we would keep turning up the music of God's love and would occasionally shout for joy!

I also spent hours reading the books Billy had written and others that were being written about him. In his classic *Peace with God*, published in 1953, he quoted from 1 Peter, characterizing the Christian's fellowship with Christ as "a joy unspeakable and full of glory."[5] He also described heaven as "a time of joy, service, laughter, singing, and praise to God." In one of his early sermons he spoke of the "desperate need" of Christians for "exuberance and vitality in their loyalty to Christ." That exuberance was what I missed in many current Christian periodicals. I found it in the New Testament and coveted it for our new magazine.

Soon huge carloads of paper began arriving at our St. Paul

*Americans in Paris: George Wilson, (left) BGEA vice president, and
the editor visit the printing plant as the first issue of* Decision
comes off the press in French in April 1963.

printer from paper mills in northern Minnesota. The printing sales-
man who handled our account told us a true story about two sales-
men from different paper companies who met in a coffee shop in
Grand Rapids, Minnesota, about this time. Naturally, one asked the
other how his business was going.

"Slow," was the reply, "except for one thing. We just got a con-
tract to deliver twelve carloads of paper every month to Billy Graham
in the Twin Cities, and it helps to beat hell!"

He spoke better than he knew.

The business office of BGEA was expanded to handle the mailing operation. Advance subscriptions began rolling in at two dollars
apiece. Excitement was in the air. On October 18, 1960, a front-page
article in the Minneapolis *Star* newspaper announced the publication
of the first issue of *Decision* magazine by the Billy Graham
Evangelistic Association. It carried photos of George Wilson, managing editor, and myself—not Billy, even though the whole thing was
his idea. Billy wired his congratulations and repeated his desire that
the praise and the glory be God's.

A group of us drove to the Jensen Printing Company plant to see
the first copies come off the press. It was a moment for reflection and
also for celebration. In the great press room my hands shook as I held

the cover page. I had chosen a dramatic picture of the Matterhorn to illustrate Billy's page one sermon, "Rising Above Conformity." But while I studied the color work, I was really reflecting on the uneven trail of my own past and thinking, *Where am I? Do I belong here?*

That night as I lay in bed, I further reflected. I reviewed the kind of writing I had done for a living as a young reporter: murder trials, police and hospital beats, divorces, football games, waterfronts, fires, embezzlements, bridge parties. I thought of the famous people I had chased after for quotes: Babe Ruth, Amelia Earhart, Cecil B. DeMille, Irving Berlin, Melvin Belli, Secretary of the Navy Claude Swanson, and the sad impoverished widow—Marguerite Carmack— whose husband in 1896 had discovered gold in the Klondike.

As a new Christian, I had always scorned those futile years spent typing inanities and dismissed the time as wasted. But now I was beginning to see their worth. Unknown to me, a greater Hand than mine had used the seven years of frustration to prepare me as a writer. In the decades ahead I could clearly distinguish truth from error and right from wrong and exalt the Lord Jesus Christ in a way pleasing to Him. The verse came to me: "Eye has not seen, nor ear heard, nor have entered into the heart of man, the things which God has pre-pared for those who love Him."[6]

I snapped on the light and looked again at the Matterhorn pic-ture on the magazine cover. During a trip to the Stony Brook School where our son was a student, I once visited with the headmaster. This great man, Dr. Frank Gaebelein, was an educator, Alpinist, musician, and devout Christian. I knew Frank had scaled the Matterhorn, and I had always wanted to hear how he did it. I confessed to him I still had a yearning to attempt it.

Frank had looked at me and smiled. "You could make it, Woody," he said. That thrilled me, but I kept quiet, knowing that I never would. Now looking at the picture of that well-nigh impossi-ble Matterhorn summit on the cover of *Decision* magazine's first issue, I felt a warm tickle somewhere in my diaphragm. "Yes, Frank, I could make it." And I had! Thank you, Billy, and thank You, Lord.

Dear Mr. Gram,

I am just 9 years old but I understand your preaching. I've been saved and boy is it fun!!!! I listen to most of your crusades. I love Jesus very much!!!

I need your lititure because I need to learn more about living a good life.

Love, !!!

Dee Calverley

Eleven

THE PRAYER BASE

~

IF ANYONE MINISTERS, LET HIM DO IT AS WITH THE
ABILITY WHICH GOD SUPPLIES, THAT IN ALL THINGS GOD MAY
BE GLORIFIED THROUGH JESUS CHRIST.

—1 PETER 4:11

What would you say," a reporter asked Billy Graham during a sit-down interview in a place that shall not be named, "if I told you I was Jesus Christ?"

Billy stared at the man for a moment and then said, according to another reporter present, "First, I would like to see your hands." Then he added, "Jesus said that when He came, He would come in glory. I'd like to see some of your glory."

This was the Billy Graham whom his religious opponents labeled the "Antichrist." A Christian editor wrote in his paper in 1957, "The New York crusade has set back the cause of evangelism for at least fifty years." A Christian educator declared that Billy was "the worst thing to happen to the Christian church in two thousand years." Another said, "He has done more harm to the cause of Christ than any living man."

Billy took such invective lightly. At first I didn't understand how he could. He continued to write friendly letters to his opponents, all of whom he knew, for they were people who earlier had supported his work. I wondered what made him do it. What made him publicly praise people who had insulted him repeatedly with abuse, lies, and innuendoes? I had watched him on television honor a man who had written a large, unpleasant book about him, insinuating that Billy was a racist, a fascist, and (of all things) impotent!

Years of friendship with Billy finally produced the only satisfying explanation for me. The answer lies in his prayer base, which is built upon the Bible. That foundation stratum of prayer, which always supports him, also enabled him to answer the reporter's question about Jesus as he did.

During the months of 1958 when the Graham team was in San Francisco, and later during the weeks in Australia and New Zealand, I spent some time (when it was appropriate) observing Billy's treatment of people and listening to his informal conversations. I found that he mixed easily with people of high and low station and never seemed to think of himself as a celebrity. Despite the obvious vigor and authority of his pulpit ministry, he personally lived in an atmosphere of quiet joy and good cheer.

For example, once when I was in their hotel room, I heard him gently teasing his wife, Ruth. There were three of us in the room. The fact that I was there on magazine business meant nothing to them at the moment. They were in love and having fun. Again, being around Billy Graham and Grady Wilson, Billy's longtime friend and associate, often would put a smile on my face.

Grady would take particular pleasure in pointing out to Billy certain grammatical slips and inconsistencies, such as his tongue tripping on the name of King Saul's grandson Mephibosheth and his mispronunciation of "nuclear" as "nucular." Billy in turn would talk before the team about the necessity of "enduring hardness as a good soldier of Jesus Christ" and then make a subtle reference to Grady's well-known girth. This kind of gentle repartee impressed me as what the church needs to offset the heavy theological atmosphere. It comes through as a good working basis for the manifesting of God's grace and love. Billy, like Nathaniel, appeared to me as a man in whom there was no guile.[1] From what I have since learned of life, I can see that such freedom comes naturally from a healthy prayer base.

My pastor, Mike MacIntosh, is a friend of Billy's. He has recently published a beautiful book, *The Tender Touch of God,* and in it he writes, "One day I asked Billy Graham about his personal prayer life.

He told me that God had taught him to pray all day long—in the shower, driving in an automobile, flying in an airplane. In fact, he said that he had been asking God for wisdom while talking to me. He wanted to know what he could say or do to encourage me. Basically, he prayed unceasingly."[2]

Once when I was on the West Coast, I learned something more about Billy's prayer base from a great intercessor, Armin Gesswein, and his wife, Reidun. Armin was a Missouri Synod Lutheran pastor who had independently organized a "Revival Prayer Fellowship" in southern California. He played a key role in Billy's 1949 tent crusade. Twelve years earlier God had used him in a massive spiritual revival in Norway. Even today, as I write, Armin is still active, although he is nearly ninety years old. The man's entire adult life has been spent teaching Christians how to pray effectively and with power in the Holy Spirit.

Armin told me in my 1961 interview with him about a historic prayer meeting twelve years earlier involving Billy Graham. The many books about Billy missed it, even though it seems to have had a significant effect on his future ministry as an evangelist. Let me tell it as Armin related it to me and as I published it in *Decision* magazine.[3]

The scene was the Westminster Hotel's Rainbow Room in Winona Lake, Indiana, and the day was Wednesday, July 13, 1949. The occasion was the fifth annual convention of Youth for Christ, a movement that had been holding Saturday night evangelistic rallies for young people across the United States and Canada and was now spreading abroad. It was three o'clock in the morning, and the young leaders of those rallies had been in that room for five hours praying.

What were they praying about? Those present said they were praying, among other things, that *God would raise up a man through whom He would bring revival*. Such a prayer was remarkably similar to the prayer of Billy Graham's father, Frank Graham, and his friends Walter Wilson and Vernon Patterson back in the days when young Billy was still milking cows. Perhaps the Youth for Christ leaders in the Rainbow Room had in mind someone like Evan Roberts, who came out of the coal mines to lead the great Welsh revival of

1904-06. Whatever their thoughts, the leaders had been meeting all week in the hotel talking evangelism, and they were dissatisfied. They yearned for more power of the Holy Spirit to be manifested. They were fully convinced that the price of leadership in ministry is *prayer*, not the peripheral prayer that Christians use to open and close meetings, but prayer (in Armin's phrase) that is "frontal." Therefore they had scheduled an all-night prayer meeting, hoping to go beyond human methods and efforts to God Himself.

At midnight Robert Cook, president of Youth for Christ, challenged the men with the words, "Who is dry? Who feels out of the will of God? Who senses that his work is fruitless?" The response was such that the meeting divided into small groups of men asking for and receiving help through individual prayer.

By three o'clock things were warming up, and as one participant described it, "the tide was running high." At that point Armin himself stood to his feet and said, "Our brother Billy Graham is going out to Los Angeles for a crusade this fall. Why don't we just gather around this man and lay our hands on him and really pray for him? Let's ask God for a fresh touch to anoint him for this work."

In response Billy rose without saying anything, walked to the front, and knelt on the oak floor. A dozen men gathered around him to lay on hands, and the intercession began.

When it was over and the men were still kneeling, Billy opened his Bible to Joel 3:13-14 and read aloud the words: "Put ye in the sickle, for the harvest is ripe: come, get you down; for the press is full, the vats overflow; for their wickedness is great. Multitudes, multitudes in the valley of decision: for the day of the Lord is near in the valley of decision" (KJV).

Billy then added, "Fellows, I'm taking that passage with me to the West Coast. I believe if we will put in the sickle, we shall reap an unprecedented harvest of souls for Christ." After that the praying continued unabated for another hour.

Three hundred years earlier Matthew Henry wrote, "When God intends great mercy on His people, He first of all sets them a-praying." The German theologians have an expression *heilsgeschicht*, which means "salvation history." From the point of view of *heils-*

geschicht, I would suggest that the Rainbow Room prayer meeting may have had more to do with Billy's evangelistic crusade in Los Angeles that autumn than all the human preparations involved. Not that there weren't thousands of other prayers going up as well! But in the counsels of heaven God has His own salvation agenda, and it just might be that the Holy Spirit was present in special power that night in Winona Lake, Indiana.

What were the results? When September 1949 came, the tent at Washington Boulevard and Hill Street in Los Angeles began to fill with people. A smaller "prayer tent" totally overflowed. Crowds reached to 6,000, then 9,000, then 15,000. The three-week campaign was extended to eight.

A man in a castle near San Simeon, California, sent the famous telegram, "Puff Graham," to the city editor of the Los Angeles *Herald-Express*, and the story broke with banners, headlines, and photographs.[4] When Billy asked a reporter why they had come, he was told, "You have been kissed by William Randolph Hearst." The Associated Press teletyped it in a lead spot to several hundred cities. *Time, Life, Newsweek,* and *Quick* magazines gave as much as four pages to it. Shanghai's Communist-censored English newspaper carried it on page one. The *London Illustrated* ran a splash of pictures and a report of a fifteen-minute transatlantic interview. The most popular picture magazine in German-speaking Switzerland featured the "gospel tent."

When Billy and Ruth Graham took the train for Minneapolis on the Monday after the closing service, the conductor treated them like celebrities. At Kansas City reporters came aboard. All this sudden fame, not because of promotion and flash bulbs, but because of God's inscrutable way of answering prayer.

Then came the welcome back to Minnesota, the great meetings in early 1950 in Boston and New England that resembled revival, the new friendship with Henry Luce of *Time* magazine, the huge crusade in Columbia, South Carolina, and the opening up of a spectacular national and worldwide outreach.

Not many observers would trace all this sudden attention to Billy Graham's personal prayers or to the prayer base of his team, but as the New Testament says, spiritual things are spiritually discerned. The Holy Spirit is a quiet monitor.

It was in Billy's personal times of prayer that two great magazines were born, *Christianity Today* in 1956 and *Decision* in 1960. I remember Billy telling me that the idea for *C.T.* came to him in the middle of the night, and he got up and plotted the whole magazine right then, even to the budget!

At the time *Decision* magazine made its first appearance in November 1960, Billy had recently completed some of the major campaigns of his career. He had spent ten weeks preaching in Africa, from Liberia on the west coast to Rhodesia in the south to Ethiopia and Egypt in the northeast, followed by a tour of cities in Israel and Switzerland. In October Billy faced one of the greatest challenges of his entire ministry during a three-week crusade in West Germany. Because of its unusual nature it will be fully treated in the next chapter.

When eternity is the issue, years, centuries, and even millennia come and go, but the work of winning souls to God never ceases. The year 1961 opened with the Graham team members reaching out to many cities of Florida in a statewide crusade effort. The meetings came to an end with three weeks of nightly ministry by Billy in the Miami Beach Convention Hall.

Now an editor at last, I arrived on the scene early to find the state of Florida turning itself inside out for Billy. State universities, churches, hotels, prison chaplains, service clubs—all wanted him. A delegation from Washington, D.C., was also on hand urging the evangelist to enter national politics.

My instructions were to attend a Saturday morning team meeting in the Biltmore Terrace Hotel at Miami Beach. I entered a room to find a friendly devotional gathering of about eighteen men, each with his Bible. Some say one prayer meeting is very much like another, but not when Billy Graham is the one in charge! Our chairs were arranged in a circle. Billy spoke to us informally about the need for increasing prayer in view of all that was taking place. He shared some verses of Scripture, and we then knelt at our chairs, each man offering a prayer in turn. This was no hurry-up prelude to a business meeting. We took our time to talk to God. Prayer was the main event.

Following prayer and a short discussion of spiritual matters, Billy mentioned that copies of the new magazine were on hand and introduced me to the team members I had not yet met. There was some good humor and laughter at this meeting but all rather low key. What kept it muted, I believe, was our awareness of the incredible size of the crowds at the nightly meetings. We were continually conscious that a holy God was at work in Florida.

The men in that meeting were impressive. Some of them had been facing large crowds around the world for a decade and had often been objects of intense press scrutiny; yet they showed no symptoms of a "star mentality." Nor did they affect a phony holiness; quite the opposite. They were quiet, well-dressed Christian gentlemen. Praying informally and protractedly on their knees seemed as natural to them as shaking hands.

It was obvious that the prayers, not just of the Graham team but of thousands of Christians throughout the state, proved a key factor in Billy's Florida crusade effort, as they had in San Francisco, Australia, New Zealand, and Indianapolis.

One January evening in 1961 I remember sitting in thirty-five-degree weather in the Tangerine Bowl in Orlando, Florida, listening to Billy preach the Gospel. I remember him saying to the crowd of 8,000 present, "The devil wants to drag you down with him into the pit of hell. He would go to any lengths, pay any price to capture your soul. But he doesn't have to, because you are willing to sell out for peanuts."

Some, perhaps, didn't appreciate that kind of talk. For others it simply may have failed to penetrate from ear to brain. But in God's Providence others who sat there shivering not only understood it, but took it to heart and thanked their Lord that someone was putting it to them straight, because it was true.

Leaving two capable newspaper friends to cover the Greater Miami crusade for *Decision*, I flew back to my duties in Minneapolis and found that amazing things were breaking out on the third floor of the Billy Graham headquarters. The first issues of *Decision* had been mailed, and now the subscriptions were pouring in, ten thousand of them a day. Cheers and whistles went up all around. When

I arrived, I was greeted with laughter. Sacks and sacks of mail had arrived from the Minneapolis post office in trucks, and two dollar checks were piling up on the tables. Many checks included larger donations to Billy's ministry. Extra personnel were hired part time to handle the deluge.

Back on the second floor I sat in my office holding the latest issue, stunned by the response. I couldn't help asking what God was saying in all this. Was He answering prayer? Whose prayer? I knew my own prayer base was still pretty unstable. Once, when we were anticipating the San Francisco crusade, I did pray all night with two other ministers. They had personal matters on their minds. One of them had an option on an island in a lake in northern California that he wanted to buy for a youth camp. I was praying earnestly that Billy Graham would come to San Francisco. My friend didn't get the island, and Billy did come to San Francisco, but I took little thought of what happened that night, as I never dreamed my intercessory skills counted for much on the heavenly market.

So while I was excited about the marvelous response to our new magazine, I was having some second thoughts about myself. I had not been as faithful in prayer as I should have been. There had been so many pressures, my efforts had been so weak, and now God's blessing was so overwhelming that I felt numb.

I remembered a story about Dwight L. Moody, the great evangelist and prayer warrior. He was on a voyage across the Atlantic in a steamer that was struck by a violent storm. As he walked the deck, a fellow passenger accosted him and wanted to know why Moody wasn't down in his stateroom praying for the ship's survival. Moody's reply was, "I'm all prayed up."[5]

Well, I wasn't. But a copy of Billy's book *Peace with God* was lying on my desk. I picked up the book and began leafing through it in a critical mood, wondering instinctively how this man, who never claimed to be a writer, could produce a book that had topped the best-seller list and would be translated into hundreds of languages.

Something caught my eye on one page. I read, "One of the characteristics of the Christian is inward joy. No matter what the circumstances, there will be a joyful heart and a radiant face. So many

Christians go around with droopy faces that give no outshining glory to God. Upon meeting a Christian, it is easy to tell whether or not he or she is a victorious, spiritual, yielded Christian. A true Christian should be relaxed and radiant, capable of illuminating and not depressing his surroundings. The Bible says, 'For the joy of the Lord is your strength.'"[6]

Amen. And this joy only comes to those who spend time talking with their Lord. That's the spirit that carried Billy through the years of criticism and opposition, meeting heavy resistance with faith in God and indestructible good cheer. What an amazing boss I had! And what a liberating Lord we all have! Beginning to feel better, I shut the book and paid a visit to the little prayer chapel to get "prayed up." The devil was not going to get me for peanuts.

Dear, Mr. Grham,

Sir, we have never met but you have done a lot for our family, Mom and Dad nevery went to church untill they heard you on TV and now they go every Sunday and Wednesday. They try to live right evething is so much better.

In Christain Love,
Kitty Wilcox

Twelve

BERLIN:
COURAGE UNDER FIRE

~

LORD, LOOK ON THEIR THREATS,
AND GRANT TO YOUR SERVANTS THAT WITH ALL
BOLDNESS THEY MAY SPEAK YOUR WORD.

—ACTS 4:29

Of all the nations on the continent of Europe, Germany has probably welcomed Billy Graham with the greatest enthusiasm. The crusades there in 1960 were no exception. After a week in Essen, capital of the Ruhr distict and home of the famed Krupp iron and steel works, with 25,000 present on opening night, the team moved on to Hamburg.[1]

The Hamburg week opened with a beautiful dedicatory service in ancient St. Michal's Cathedral, conducted by Bishop Holstein. On the first night the specially erected crusade tent was hopelessly overcrowded; there were more people standing around it than were seated inside. A *Die Welt* reporter described the scene inside the crusade tent:

> The 35,000 are so quiet that one can hear his neighbor breathe. And then something happens which had not been expected in Hamburg. Suddenly the free space between the platform and the front row is filled to capacity. Many men are there, many young men. What is happening inside of them—in their hearts? But this is indeed no one's business. It is said there were 4,000 who had come to the front. In no city, it is

said, were there so many. It happened in Hamburg. Does one know his city? Does one know his neighbor?

The most unusual meeting in Hamburg took place late at night at the entrance to the Reeperbahn, Hamburg's notorious underground section. Ten thousand standees gathered to hear a Billy Graham sermon drawn from theater marquee titles. Beggars, pimps, prostitutes, bar girls, ex-convicts, assorted toughs all stood listening as Billy told them, "All of you are searching for something. In Hamburg the nights are long, but much longer is the night if there is sin in your heart."

The Graham team's last stop was Berlin, the island capital then surrounded by Communist territory on all sides. They arrived less than a year before Nikita Khrushchev ordered the erection of the infamous Berlin Wall. That week in Berlin may rank as the greatest external test of Billy's long ministry. In my opinion it brought to the surface bravery and hidden strength of character in the evangelist in the face of extreme danger and showed the world for all time what God will do for a man of prayer. It also brought out the finest qualities of courage in the Christian citizenry of free Germany.

The people of Berlin had heard Billy before. Because of his emphatic way of speaking, they had affectionately nicknamed him "Gottes Machinengewehr" (God's machine gun). The crusade committee had designed and erected a huge elongated tent and pitched it on the Square of the Republic, just 300 yards from the East German border. A West Berlin newspaper published a clever cartoon that had an East German guard commenting on Billy's preaching tent: "If every machine gun on our side had a tent over it, the whole Republic would look like a camping ground!" The tent capacity was 20,000 seats, and when the Berlin meetings began, it proved too small.

The East Berlin police responded to Billy Graham's arrival by giving him "twenty-four hours in which to get out of town." The Communist newspaper *Neues Deutschland* described Billy as a "religious charlatan" and declared that he had been seen in Paris escorting a blonde described as "one Beverly Shea!" The lord mayor of East Berlin labeled Billy "a representative of the Cold War by order of

NATO." Crusade Chairman Wilhelm Brauer promptly sent the lord mayor a German edition of Billy's *Peace with God*.

The East German government warned that all kinds of reprisals would follow this "crude provocation" and demanded that the tent be moved. Mayor Willi Brandt refused. Billy Graham's reaction was to preach his first sermon in the crowded tent on John 3:16 and to read greetings to the German Christians from the president of the Evangelical Baptist Union of Moscow, USSR! Wisely, he refused to attack communism directly.

East German tanks and water cannons soon rolled up to the Brandenburg Gate, pointed threateningly at the tent. At least one tank fired a shot during an afternoon Bible class taught by Roy Gustafson of the Graham team. West Berlin officials quickly dispatched a fire truck, special details, and police dogs to the crusade tent.

At the Brandenburg Gate scores of "vopos" (*Volks polizei* or people's police) harassed the hundreds of East Berliners seeking to come through the gate each night to attend the meetings, and police managed to bar many. (Most of the 1000-voice choir came from East Berlin.) At other entrances to West Berlin, people were pulled off subways, frisked, harassed, and ridiculed. The "vopos" ripped crusade posters from the walls of the subway and elevated train stations controlled by East Berlin.

Yet night after night, in spite of everything, the people came from east and west in forty-degree weather, and for one glorious week the Gospel was proclaimed in the Square of the Republic, just 300 yards from the fateful boundary between two worlds.

Billy told the East Berlin people who came forward at his meetings to give their pastors' names, but not to give their own addresses to the counselors, lest they should be persecuted in the follow-up.

One morning 25,000 teenagers gathered in the great square, the tent proving too small. They heard a summons to make a personal decision on moral and spiritual issues. Such a ministry was new on the German religious scene.

For a change, the German pastors one evening requested the omission of the traditional invitation music. They wanted to see whether the response would be as great without the emotional impact of the choir singing "Just As I Am." That night more people came forward than the night before!

The final Sunday afternoon service was held outdoors on a warm October day in front of a burned-out shell that had been the Reichstag (capitol) building before Hitler set fire to it. It stood just a stone's throw from the East Berlin border at the Brandenburg Gate, where hundreds of "vopos" stood ready. "Vopos" also patrolled the railroad track that divided the Soviet from the Western sector, and hundreds of East Berliners, unable to cross, stood along the track and listened over a wire fence to the brass band of 150 instruments and Billy's gospel message by public address.

What a sight! Ninety thousand Germans gathered before the Reichstag that closing Sunday afternoon, and most of them stood through the entire service. Beyond the Brandenburg Gate on the Unter den Linden Boulevard, others who were barred from attending strained to catch the message of God's Word over the speakers.

Billy Graham told the great crowd in words translated by Peter Schneider:

> If Germany opens its heart and mind to Christ, it could once again lead the whole world spiritually. We stand at the center of history in front of this historic Reichstag. My plea to you today is that you come to a strong belief in the Bible as the Word of God. Martin Luther was reading this book when God spoke to him. You come back to this book, begin to read it, study it, and God will speak to you, and through you perhaps history can again be changed. Young people of this generation cannot remember much about the war. They are searching for something to believe in—a slogan, a flag, a leader to follow. Let that leader be Christ.

When the call came for a decision, the space at the front of the podium in the large square could not accommodate all who wished to respond. Counselors had to mingle with the throng to reach the inquirers.

The crusade closed with 90,000 voices singing Martin Luther's stirring hymn, *"Ein feste Burg ist unser Gott"* ("A Mighty Fortress Is Our God"). Citizens of the West returned to their homes in the tense island city, humming another popular crusade tune, "Jesus Is Coming." Meanwhile visitors from the East slipped back across the sector boundary, some escaping detection, others being seized for the inevitable interrogation and harassment.

Not until twenty-nine more years had passed did relief come to East Berlin. Finally in in 1989 prayers were answered, the pressure eased, the Wall collapsed, and full, glorious freedom came once again to reunite the brave men and women and children of East and West Berlin.

Dear Mr. Grahm

I've only seen two of your specials but since then I've come very close to God. I'd like very much to read the Book you advertised on your special. I am thirteen and I just lost my mother and this allso brought me closer to God then one night I thougth to my self. Vicki You have no Mother You have no father But you allways have God, So stop pitying your self.

Love Vicki

Thirteen

MISSING ON MOUNT SHASTA

~

I WILL LIFT UP MY EYES TO THE HILLS—FROM WHENCE COMES
MY HELP? MY HELP COMES FROM THE LORD.

—PSALM 121:1-2

In *Decision* magazine's second year of publication, I received a note
from my close friend Grady Wilson, who had already rescued me
from more than one exigency. Sometimes I think God gave us friends
to turn the wheels of creation. I'm sure friends are a great part of
what life is all about. Grady was obviously feeling good on May 18,
1962, as he wrote me the following letter from Charlotte, North
Carolina:

> *Dear Woody:*
> *You are doing a bang-up job with Decision Magazine.*
> *Everywhere I go, people are commenting on your masterful*
> *presentation. Coming back from Florida, Billy remarked*
> *about how you were God's man for this job. Keep it up and*
> *more power to you! We love you much and thank God that*
> *He sent you our way.*
>
> > *Your devoted friend,*
> > *Grady*

Can you imagine working for people like that?

Two months later Grady was driving down the Bayshore
Freeway south of San Francisco early one morning in July. Seated

next to him again was Billy Graham. The two evangelists had spent the night in the Villa Motor Hotel, San Mateo, and were now heading for Fresno. There on the following day Billy would be holding a press conference in advance of his eight-day crusade in Ratcliffe Stadium.

Exciting plans had been made by Crusade Director Bill Brown and his staff to reach out to the entire San Joaquin Valley with the message of Jesus Christ. They expected that thousands of people would fill the stadium where Australian John Landy had run the first under-four-minute mile ever recorded in the United States.

Counselors were being recruited who could speak German, Swedish, Russian, and Chinese. A young Argentine named Luis Palau, a student at Multnomah School of the Bible, was appointed translator for the special Spanish-speaking section.

At nine o'clock that morning Grady Wilson turned on the car radio to pick up the CBS newscast. The first news item stated that the sheriff of Siskiyou County had listed an aide of Evangelist Billy Graham named Sherwood Wirt as missing on Mount Shasta, a 14,161-foot snow-covered peak in northern California.

According to Grady's account, Billy commanded in alarm, "Stop the car! We've got to find him! We'll get a dog team."

"I can't stop the car; we're on the freeway," protested Grady.

They drove into San Jose where they pulled off and found a telephone. Billy called his headquarters in Minneapolis.

According to Billy's story, which he told at the Fresno press conference next day and which I have on tape, he said, "I asked myself two questions: first, why he was up there, and second, what happened? I told the people in Minneapolis, 'Get the finest search parties, and we're going to try to get a plane right now and go up and see if we can find him.'"

Billy had recently come from an exhaustive tour of the western countries of South America and would shortly be preaching his way down the eastern side. He had spent several days in May proclaiming Christ to 700,000 citizens of Chicago. A climactic rally in Soldier Field drew a crowd of 116,000, according to the Chicago *Tribune*. He quickly followed that crusade with another huge rally at the

World's Fair in Seattle. The eight days in July he spent in Fresno were sandwiched in between a schedule that would exhaust any but the stoutest physical specimen.

Now Billy was proposing to vacate Fresno, despite all the preparations made by hundreds of volunteers and prayer warriors, and fly off to the slopes of Mount Shasta looking for one of his employees who had gotten into trouble while off duty. If you think Mr. Graham was just pretending or striking a pose, you don't know the gentleman.

My own story of "what happened" is fairly easy to relate. "Why I was up there" is a bit more involved. I tell it only to illustrate Graham's response to my predicament.

Not being able to take normal vacations due to the task of producing twelve issues a year of *Decision*, I had fudged slightly on my reporting assignment in Fresno. Leaving Minneapolis two days early, I rented a Volkswagen "Beetle" in San Francisco and drove to Mount Shasta City. There I spent a whole day trying to enlist a hiker willing to scale the mountain with me. Being unsuccessful, I drove to the ski lodge, parked my car, and rode the lift (since destroyed by an avalanche) to the ski shack at the 9,300-foot elevation.

Why did I want to climb this mountain? Because I was brought up in the Berkeley hills and had spent the last two years in prairie country. I yearned to climb. I felt drawn to this mountain because it is magnificent and because God has often talked to people on mountains. William Blake stated it well:

> *Great things are done when men and mountains meet;*
> *This is not done by jostling in the street.*[1]

Our father Abraham met God on a mountain. So did Moses and the author of Psalms 42 and 121. So did Peter, James, and John. Our Lord talked to His Father on a mountain. He taught on a mountain, departed this earth from a mountain, and when He returns, it will be on a mountain.

Starting from the Mount Shasta ski shack at 3 AM, I passed the Red Rocks six hours later by using crampons on my feet. By 11 AM

I was at the foot of Misery Hill, and at 2:15 I arrived at the crater summit, 14,161 feet. Descending, I slid down the snow patches for several miles and overshot the point where I had entered Avalanche Gulch from the ski lift. For a short time I really was lost. An hour of difficult climbing brought me to the head of the ski lift at 8 PM just as the sun was setting.

I knew the lift ceased operating at 5 PM. I did not know that the attendant had turned in my calling card to the sheriff's office. While I spent the night in the ski shack, a local AP correspondent took my name off the sheriff's blotter, and next day virtually every newspaper in the United States knew that Billy Graham's "aide" was "lost"— except in Minneapolis where the papers were on strike.

But I wasn't lost. Another saw to that. I came down in the lift next morning and found that the sheriff had driven up to the lodge earlier looking for me. Fortunately I missed him, and next day I came to Billy Graham's press conference in Fresno. My boss greeted me: "Sherwood Wirt walked in a moment ago. Sherwood, would you stand? We've been worried about him. He's the fellow that's been lost on Mount Shasta . . ." (laughter) Billy went on to describe his plans for a dramatic rescue and then added, "While we were on the phone to Minneapolis, the other phone rang, and they said, 'Well, he's been found.' So we're delighted to have you here. I hope you enjoyed your experience. You gave a lot of us heart failure."

It was God who brought me off Mount Shasta safely but exhausted. I barely made it. No one should climb that peak alone, particularly if he is fifty-one years old. But I do not tell the incident to make a witness. My fellow team member Norman Pell likes to say, "I never know whether God is guiding my decisions or overruling my mistakes." The story is included principally for what it reveals about the man I love to call Boss.

What manner of man is Billy Graham? Dr. Iremonger, biographer of Archbishop William Temple, tried to explain *his* subject's spiritual acumen by saying that he had a "low threshold between his conscious and unconscious self," so that his soul expressed itself more spontaneously than is usual in people, and thoughts of unusual wisdom and perceptivity came easily.[2] The same might be applied to Graham.

Islanders of the South Pacific claim that Billy has "mana," a kind of mysterious but powerful stuff that they say clings to unique individuals and makes them poets or geniuses or witch doctors or dictators—or evangelists. I prefer to speak of the anointing of the Holy Spirit, which is God's special preparation of a man or woman who has been uniquely set apart for His work.

I prefer simply to sum it all up and call it greatness.

Of all the Billy Graham crusades I have attended around the globe, Fresno 1962 remains my favorite. It was like a delightful lawn party with balmy evenings, Spirit-filled music, strong preaching, and lovely people of every description attending. I will always remember the hundreds of Old Mennonite sisters with their bonnets, the German Baptist preachers with their beards, and the God-fearing farmers and orchard men with their families.

Fresno is the queen city of the richest agricultural area on earth (raisin grapes, peaches, apricots, figs, and melons in abundance as well as grains), but the nightly crowds came to Ratcliffe from far beyond the San Joaquin Valley. Buses rolled in nightly from Los Angeles, San Francisco, Yosemite and Kings Canyon National Parks in the Sierra Nevadas, and waypoints—including Ceres, where Cliff Barrows was born. Six hundred singing passengers arrived each night by special train from Bakersfield, 100 miles away. There were "incurables" from Fresno General Hospital who stayed in their bus and a paralytic woman who wrote sermons with a pencil in her teeth. And everywhere there were teenagers.

But it was no picnic. Billy's sermons were a sharp warning of judgment to come, a trumpet call to repentance, and a gracious invitation to eternal life through Jesus Christ. And when the invitation was extended, they came, hundreds of them every night, seeking salvation, restitution, and new life from the Savior of the world. Among them were a senior theological student from Berkeley and an Iraqi student from Baghdad who was counseled in Arabic.

A minister in Porterville in the Sierra foothills wrote afterward to *Decision* ordering forty subscriptions. He added this note:

> *The good that our church received from the Fresno meetings was immeasurable, and the help that I received personally was the greatest thing that has happened in my life.*
>
> *We sponsored a thirty-nine-passenger bus to Fresno each night, a distance of seventy-five miles. Transportation was free to anyone who wanted to go. We had to use one to six cars to take care of the overflow. Monday night we had eighteen teenagers on the bus, and sixteen made commitments. Wednesday night we had an overload of sixty-nine passengers.*
>
> *It was something to hear the young people's conversation on the way home from the meetings—their concern for others and their making lists of their friends whom they were going to call so they would attend the meetings.*

Whether the congregation was large or small, Episcopal or Pentecostal, church support for the crusade was fabulous in the Fresno area. More than one pastor was astonished when scores of referral cards of inquirers arrived in his mailbox. Two local television channels carried the crusade for six nights following.

Like Samaria after the apostle Philip had preached Christ to the people, there was great joy in Fresno in the days after the meetings closed.

And Billy?

He was at home with Ruth and his family in North Carolina, getting ready for a fall preaching tour of Sao Paulo, Asuncion, Cordoba, Rosario, Montevideo, and Buenos Aires, and a November crusade in El Paso, Texas.

Fourteen

WRITE THE VISION

~

I WAS IN THE SPIRIT ON THE LORD'S DAY, AND I
HEARD BEHIND ME A LOUD VOICE, AS OF
A TRUMPET, SAYING . . . WRITE. . . .

—REVELATION 1:10-11

Seated on a camp chair under a coconut palm tree on the shore of Hilo Bay, Hawaii, opposite Coconut Island, I began typing my first book. The year was 1933, and I was twenty-two years old. My desk was a fruit crate on which reposed a seventeen-dollar portable typewriter. The manuscript was titled *The Glory Hole,* and it described realistically and saucily the life of a deck boy aboard a seagoing Matson Line sugar freighter. I intended it to be my passport into the literary world of Alec Waugh and W. Somerset Maugham, but the Writer in the Sky intended otherwise. The yellowing manuscript is still in my file.

Other attempts at writing books met the same fate: a narrative about a rowboat trip on the Yukon River, a church history essay titled *Pioneers of Faith in Action,* and even a doctoral dissertation that won a degree but failed to make it into print.

Not until twenty-six years had passed did my first genuine, authentic, professional hardback come off the press of Harper & Brothers in 1959. Its title? *Crusade at the Golden Gate.* Its subject? Billy Graham. Who marketed it? Friends of Billy Graham. On the fly-leaf Billy wrote, "To Sherwood Wirt, with deep appreciation for this contribution to our ministry and the Kingdom of God. Billy Graham,

Philippians 1:6." Norman Vincent Peale wrote me that he considered it the finest book written about Billy to date.

So began at long last a literary career that under God has included writing and publishing over two dozen books, editing many others, and producing a magazine for Billy Graham that set records in Christian publishing, while expanding its own outreach to ten issues in five foreign languages (French, German, Spanish, Japanese, and Chinese) and Braille.[1]

During *Decision*'s first year of publication, our growth was phenomenal, but so were my editorial problems. Good contemporary material, I discovered, was hard to find. Writers were inundating us with testimonies, poetry, and stories about their hospital stays, but it was mostly unusable.

In December 1961, three Minnesota writers invited my wife and me to accompany them to a Christian writers' conference in Chicago, and I came back with a secret agenda. It was to establish a writers' seminar that would teach God's people how to write top-grade, highly readable material for the market, including *Decision*. And there was something more.

In meeting with writers and aspiring writers, I had made a pitiful discovery. Many of them were making the same mistakes in dealing with publishers that I had made for twenty-five years. Thanks to Billy Graham, I had learned at last how a writer can get his or her material into print, and I wanted to share that with them. Especially I wanted them to stop wasting their time and postage sending off manuscripts to unknown outlets.

In January 1962, Billy summoned his team to a meeting at the Biltmore Terrace Hotel in Miami Beach, and I was included. When my turn came to give a brief report of my ministry, I told the team my plan while I stood facing Billy. I said the devotional material being submitted to us at *Decision* was not what the Christians I knew wanted to read in the 1960s. They wanted fresh, lively, captivating articles and testimonies that reflected scriptural truth, that were not above using humor, and that spoke directly to the reader's condition with a victorious message of faith and hope and love.

Then I said that I wanted to inaugurate a school of Christian writing that would produce writers who would contribute choice material to our magazine. I proposed to hold it at the Billy Graham headquarters in Minneapolis. As I sat down, I noticed that Billy was smiling.

Later I spoke to him, and he said simply, "Draw up a plan and send it to me." I soon learned that Billy was different from other evangelists in one significant way: he understood the value of the written word in bringing people to Christ. He was not solely verbal, or as Disraeli said of Gladstone, "inebriated with the exuberance of his own verbosity."

Billy Graham was in fact deeply committed to literary evangelism and had already written *Peace with God* and *The Secret of Happiness,* two excellent books that became bestsellers and were translated into scores of languages, including Russian. His crusade sermons and radio messages were also printed and mailed out daily as tracts, and he was starting a daily syndicated column titled "My Answer," which still appears today in many newspapers.

Here is a partial list of Billy's books to date:
America's Hour of Decision, 1951
Peace with God, 1953
The Secret of Happiness, 1955
My Answer, 1960
World Aflame, 1965
The Challenge, 1969
The Jesus Generation, 1971
Angels, 1975
How to Be Born Again, 1977
The Holy Spirit, 1978
Till Armageddon, 1981
Approaching Hoofbeats, 1983
A Biblical Standard for Evangelists, 1984
Unto the Hills, 1986
Facing Death and the Life After, 1987
Answers to Life's Problems, 1988
Hope for the Troubled Heart, 1991
Storm Warning, 1992
Just As I Am (Memoirs), 1997

It was Billy's determination to proclaim the Gospel by the written word that brought into being *Christianity Today* and *Decision*. Not every evangelist has chosen the literary route. Some seem to have a great reluctance to sit down and write a paragraph. Life for them is verbal rather than literary. They listen to tapes, but read few books other than the Bible. They quote to me Paul's remark in his letter to the Romans: "How shall they hear without a preacher?"[2]

I agree that Paul certainly favored preaching, and yet I remind writers that it is what Paul *wrote*, rather than what he preached verbally, that has come down to us. He himself admitted that his letters were more powerful than his sermons. Perhaps he knew—certainly the Holy Spirit knew—that if it were not for the written word of Scripture, today's church would have nothing to preach. Preaching is vital—always has been and always will be until Jesus returns. Electronics have augmented preaching and made it even more significant. But we should never underestimate the power of the written word.

When I returned to Minneapolis, I found that not everyone at the Billy Graham headquarters favored my idea of a school of writing. We had no dormitory facilities and no auditorium. "Anyway," I was asked, "what has a writing school to do with evangelism?"

Nevertheless, in July 1963, some ninety writers enrolled in the first three-day Decision School of Christian Writing. Our *Decision* staff made up the entire faculty, with one addition. I read a message of greeting sent from North Carolina by Billy Graham. We held some workshops on stairwells and ate meals at odd hours and paid our way. As for those who attended, they were totally enthusiastic and promised to come back next year, which they did in larger numbers.

A couple of years later, unknown to us, the heiress to an industrial fortune attended one of our writing schools as a registrant. We gave her the same courteous treatment we gave everybody who came to the school. She went home so delighted that when she wrote her thanks, she enclosed a generous gift to the ministry of the Billy Graham Association. After that I heard no questions about the evangelistic value of writing seminars! Meanwhile the Holy Spirit kept blessing the incoming mail department with new subscriptions, and readers continued to write us saying in different ways that they had found Jesus Christ as their Savior and Lord through the pages of the magazine. The subscription list to *Decision* increased until our monthly press run peaked at 5,285,000 copies, making it the largest Christian magazine in the world.

In the years since 1963, Christian writing seminars have burgeoned, spreading over America and the entire world under different auspices but all serving the same Lord. I have taught such schools in Alaska, Canada, several countries of Europe, South America, South Africa, and all around the Pacific Rim. Billy Graham may not fully realize it, but his interest in literary evangelism was a primary impetus in starting it all.

On an airplane trip from Auckland to Sydney, I had the pleasure of sharing with Ruth and Billy Graham, at their request, some of the principles I still use in teaching fellow writers. The Grahams, of course, are both brilliant writers, and each has had an amazing literary output. I have no doubt that their books will not only be on the shelves until the Lord returns, but will be taken down and read repeatedly.

And what is it that I tell Christians who write and want to become published? I ask four questions:

1. *Motivation.* Why do you wish to write? Ambition? Pride? Money? Christ offers a better motive.

2. *Contacts.* Getting into print is like getting into heaven: It's not what you do; it's whom you know.

3. *Discipline.* Write something every day. Then join a critique group and rewrite it.

4. *Tools.* Whatever you need. Ask your family to stop giving you neckties and sweaters for Christmas and instead give you tools for writing.

THE WHEAT HEADS

~

*Important steps: Inquirers cross from stadium bleachers to turf
as they respond to Graham's invitation.*

~ STEPS TO HEAVEN ~

Hammer hammer hammer
   stadium crew
six hours to go
   so much to do.
Fresh clean lumber
   ten-penny nails
Steps to Jesus
   with handrails.
Steps to the green turf
   sacred sod
home of the Giants
   home of God.
Thousands coming
   to hear the man
offering Jesus
   God's great plan.
Walk ye the way
   walk ye the walk
Christ wants action
   not just talk.
Test those risers
   make them hold,
I have a son
   twenty years old;
He needs help
   and he just might
walk these steps
   to heaven tonight.

—S. E. W.

Mr. Graham,
Well Mr Graham I am writing this to you,
telling you that God is a big (?)
                                                To me.
    I am 16 years full of sin. Almost 17 by this
coming 26th of June.
    I drink, smoke, some time sniff all the
things that make you "Trip".
    I know these things make you deeper, and darker
in sin But I perform these acts, knowing that they
are wrong. Why? I ask my self.
    And then later, I would feel dum, stupid and all
other things that make you feel like that, knowing that
they were wrong!!!
    To tell you the truth, I even forced My self to
write this letter. I think I know Im doing the
right thing.
    To tell you even more I will even make
more and more sins I KNOW I WILL !!!
Because I ain't got what you have.
        I KNOW that most of me is
            Negative(-) Not Positive(+)
            (bad)   (good)

Please send me all That stuff !!!
That makes it so Tuff.
To Believe in your Stuff.

                    C.R.

Fifteen

EASTER IN
BIRMINGHAM

~

BLESSED BE THE LORD GOD, THE GOD OF ISRAEL,
WHO ONLY DOES WONDROUS THINGS.

—PSALM 72:18

Late in March 1964, I rode with Billy and one or two colleagues from the Billy Graham Minneapolis headquarters to the Twin Cities International Airport to give our boss a send-off. Billy had an Easter preaching date in Birmingham, Alabama, on March 29 that promised to be history-making, and we wanted to offer him our prayers and support. What brought it all about was an issue as complex as it was volatile.

A reporter from the St. Paul *Post-Dispatch* joined us at the airport, and Billy gave him a brief interview as we stood in the waiting room. The reporter asked a highly significant question: "When people come forward at your meeting seeking salvation, will you permit black counselors to talk to the white inquirers and pray with them?"

In 1964 black Christians still did not customarily counsel white people at evangelistic gatherings in the southern part of the United States. White Christians accepted such a custom as normal behavior, feeling it would avoid "giving offense" to the inquirers.

I heard Billy's simple answer: "Our counselors will be instructed to conduct themselves toward inquirers in Birmingham in the same way as they have always been instructed in our meetings all over the world. There will be no difference." Period!

Birmingham in 1964 was the leading industrial city of the south. From the day of its founding in 1870, the steel metropolis had been divided racially. Blacks were considered inferior and were treated as such by the governing authority. By the end of World War II, during which American Negro troops performed with exceptional valor, attitudes were changing. Voices in the south clamored increasingly for a breakdown of racial barriers and an end to inequality in the official treatment of black and white citizens.

"Separate-but-equal" schools for blacks had been outlawed by the U.S. Supreme Court in 1954. The tragic bombing of Birmingham's Sixteenth Street Baptist Church in September 1963 killed four black Sunday school children. No perpetrators were ever found, but an outcry of protest rang out across the nation. The civic leaders and power brokers of Birmingham, as well as much of the white citizenry, knew that something had to be done. America was now different. A change in racial policy was overdue.

The leaders knew very well that their city should abolish discriminatory civic laws, but they wondered how and when to do it. During this period Billy Graham made a gracious offer to come to the city and conduct an evangelistic rally on Easter Sunday in 1964. The clergy as a whole favored his coming, and the civic leaders thought, *Why not do it then?* Billy was popular in Birmingham (as everywhere else), and his services had been integrated for years. The churches of Birmingham were urged to accept Billy's offer to conduct an integrated evangelistic rally in Legion Field similar to those he had led around the world. The city fathers believed correctly that such a meeting would relieve tension in the populace. Separate drinking fountains, separate toilets, separate seating in public places, and other symbols of government-approved discrimination would then quietly disappear.

To their credit, the civic leaders and pastors saw Billy's Easter Sunday offer as a way to introduce integration on a high spiritual note. They planned the God-honoring rally as the first desegregated public gathering in Birmingham's history.

On March 28, the day before Easter, I arrived in Birmingham in time to attend a reception for the team. Some of the crusade committee members were present, and I had the pleasure of meeting the Reverend J. L. Ware. He was a prominent committeeman and pastor of Trinity Baptist Church, one of the largest black churches in the city. It was clear that Birmingham's black community was identifying solidly with Billy Graham and his ministry.

Billy's own record spoke for itself. His meetings had open seating. He had traveled to Brazil in company with Dr. Martin Luther King, Jr., and had invited Dr. King to lead in prayer at the 1957 crusade in New York City's Madison Square Garden. Two dedicated black evangelists, Dr. Howard Jones and Dr. Ralph Bell, were members of his evangelistic team and were preaching everywhere.

As Dr. Ware and I chatted informally, I mentioned to him that I had served as chaplain to colored troops in World War II (before desegregation of the military) and would love to visit his church.[1] He politely told me I would be welcome.

Going to Birmingham took courage on Billy's part. It was by no means clear that Birmingham's white community as a whole approved the new policy. On the day before Easter, the city was extremely tense. Memories of lynchings were not that old. In common conversation people voiced fears of a race riot. Followers of Malcolm X uttered threats. A segregated "Citizens' Council" demanded the rally's cancellation. Some churchgoers, fearful of danger, planned to avoid the crusade rally at Legion Field.

I awoke early on Easter morning, dressed, and went to the hotel lobby. There I learned that several officers on motorcycles were policing the highway between the city center and Legion Field and had made some arrests of young black citizens, mostly for speeding.

At about nine o'clock I set out on foot with my Bible for Pastor Ware's church. I can't explain why I went, but I knew I had to go. The streets were suspiciously empty. I was fearful, but not because of the police I might meet or the racial problems I might encounter. I was fearful because I did not wish to do anything that would somehow embarrass Billy or hurt his ministry.

Working for a world-famous person has its risks. The rule in the Minneapolis office was very strict: don't create problems for Dr. Graham. If you have a problem, work it out yourself. He has problems much greater than yours. I accepted that rule, for I believed in my heart that I was called to help Billy with his God-given mission and not to tax him with my behavior.

Timidly I found my way to the church, a huge old wooden structure. I climbed a great many steps and found the doors shut. I knocked, and one door opened a crack.

"May I come in?" I asked the usher.

"Go around back," the man pointed with his thumb and closed the door.

Descending the steps, I walked around to the back of the church. All was still; no one was in sight. It seemed that even the air was electric with fear. I remembered reading how the dreaded "egbo," a mysterious horror, swept through the West African forests where missionary Mary Slessor had launched her solo mission, spreading death and terrifying Ibo women and children until Mary defied it.[2] Whatever was in the air in Birmingham, I defied it.

I went up the back steps, a door opened, and there was Pastor Ware welcoming me inside with a smile. I could hear the congregation singing a gospel tune. "Take a seat here in the vestibule for a few minutes," said the pastor. Mounting a step or two, he opened a door and disappeared into the sanctuary.

Baffled, I squirmed on a bench for several minutes while the singing continued. This was not what I wished. I had no statement to make. I was not there to represent Billy Graham. I just wanted to come to church anonymously as a lover of Jesus and worship in a back pew with fellow Christians and then leave. In fact, I was ready to leave now.

Suddenly Pastor Ware appeared and held open the door. "Brother," he said, "the pulpit is yours!"

Mine? What did he mean? With my head swimming and my mind blank, I walked into the sanctuary and sat on the platform as the singing continued.

What I said from the pulpit that morning after being introduced is pretty much a vacuity. I know that I spoke again of my Air Force chaplaincy with colored troops in the segregated "Squadron C" at Hamilton Field, California, nineteen years earlier. I probably told

Moment in Birmingham: Alabama's largest city breaks the color bar in 1964 as Graham preaches at a giant integrated Easter rally.

them how we converted an empty barracks into a well-attended chapel and how a "GI" artist painted a dark-complexioned Jesus on the wall behind the communion table. On Sunday evenings I used military vehicles to take black soldiers to church services.[3] I do actually remember telling them that the Congregational church in which I was brought up in California continually preached on love and friendship between black and white people, and practiced it, and that the church's message had sunk deep into my heart as a boy and never left.

What Scripture I used, what Easter message I brought, if any, I have forgotten. After all, I was just a visitor to the church. But you can be sure I told them that Billy Graham was a friend who loved them, and in the name of the risen Christ, I invited them all to come out that afternoon to hear Billy preach the Gospel in Legion Field. I said they would find a warm welcome and that the seating was open to all.

As I was finishing and before I sat down, I watched a tiny girl in her Sunday dress toddle out into the aisle and come toward me. She was holding up her hand as if to greet me. I was on an elevated three-foot platform and had to come to the edge and stoop down to take her hand, which I did. She smiled. If she said something, I didn't catch it.

While I was bending over, another little girl came up waving her hand at me—then another child, a little boy. I looked up and saw children leaving their parents and coming from every direction to where I was standing, two dozen or more. They clustered around me smiling. In a long lifetime, it was the most beautiful expression of love I have ever seen. My eyes filled; I could not speak; and still they came.

At last I finished shaking hands with the little ones and sat down, an emotional wreck. I don't remember what happened after that. I believe the pastor must have stepped to the podium and thanked the children and their parents and then delivered his message.

Later that day I made my way to Legion Field. On the track surrounding the turf, I saw policemen in uniform and state troopers in plainclothes stationed every ten feet. They remained there during the service and the invitation. No one seemed to pay attention to them, for it was a wonderful Easter afternoon of peace and joy, and even the officers seemed to have a good time. The singing, the

Cliff Barrows leads the choir at the 1964 Birmingham rally.

preaching of the Gospel, the whole atmosphere was like a foretaste of heaven.

The world took note of what happened that day in Alabama's chief city. The international press carried the news that the largest interracial crowd in the history of the state had met and dispersed without incident. Columns were devoted to the racial harmony in the choir, the corps of ushers, and the platform party, which included members of the city council.

Billy Graham told the crowd, "It is a wonderful thing to gather together like this in the city of Birmingham, in the name of Jesus Christ, on Easter Day. Somehow all our problems and difficulties seem not quite so great when we stand at the foot of the cross and hear Him say, 'Father, forgive them, for they do not know what they do.'"[4]

All this happened over three decades ago. Nearly 35,000 people were present that day, and 4,000 of them came down from the stands of Legion Field to commit their lives to Christ. One of them, a fifteen-year-old white girl, later wrote to Billy Graham, "I hope you will be able to come again to Birmingham for a longer crusade. I believe if more people down here would turn to Christ, all their feelings of prejudice against the Negro would leave them. Mine have. Thank you for everything."

My guess is that no one who was there in that noble, historic southern city and who is still alive in the nineties has ever forgotten the Easter afternoon in 1964 when the name of God was lifted up by the multitudes at Legion Field, where by the grace of God, Billy Graham broke the color bar at Birmingham forever.

Growl
Growl
Growl
Need God.
Growl
Growl
Growl
Need God.
Need Bible.
Read
Read
Read
Peace

Dan Crawford

Sixteen

GOD IN
EARLS COURT

~

OH, SING TO THE LORD A NEW SONG! FOR HE
HAS DONE MARVELOUS THINGS.

—PSALM 98:1

Early in February 1966, when all hands were busily preparing for
the gigantic June Greater London Crusade, Billy Graham telephoned me in Minneapolis. "We need to get millions of people praying for London," he said. "I want you to fly over there and see what
kind of preparations are being made. Then come back and spread the
word in *Decision*. We want to get everybody in the American and
Canadian churches and the people on our mailing list praying that
God will pour out His Holy Spirit on Britain."

What an assignment and what a challenge! When I arrived in
London, I found a beehive of activity being generated from two
offices—the crusade office in Piccadilly, headed by Bill Brown of the
team, and the editorial office of Billy's newspaper *The Christian*, a
mile away, headed by its editor, Dr. J. D. Douglas.

London, the ancient city of Londinium built by Roman troops in
the first century A.D. on the banks of the Thames River, was being
prepared for the closest thing to revival since the days of Moody and
Sankey. The city itself was a fascinating sight. Old churches that had
been standing on corners for centuries, ministering to a hardy few,
were coming to life and opening their doors wide. Gallons of tea were

served as Christians showed up off the street offering to "do something." They stayed to pray.

Robert and Lois Ferm of the team had spent two years alerting churches and pastors of Britain about the crusade and were even beginning to talk with an English accent! The city's clergymen predicted a "spiritual hurricane." Prayers for the crusade were offered at ministers' fraternals, ministers' wives' meetings, youth rallies, sacred concerts, film showings, television appearances, training sessions for personal workers, choir rehearsals, ushers' meetings, Christian Life and Witness classes, and meetings in schools and industrial plants. Mini-crusades using closed-circuit television from Earls Court were being set up to take the message of salvation to ten major cities of England and Scotland.

Attractive posters adorned the double-deck buses and the billboards, inviting the public to the coming meetings. Hundreds of men's prayer meetings went into action in industrial plants and other places of work. Thousands of "cottage prayer meetings" were being formed by women who said they were planting them "on every street in London." The number actually reached 9,000.

The person in charge, Mrs. Jean Rees, wife of Evangelist Tom Rees, was a fireball. She told her ladies, "Put the chairs in a circle . . . coffee and a biscuit to begin . . . then a little 'praise talk,' thanking God, and then to the issue. . . . No nonsense now about verbal participation; if you can talk, you can pray. . . . Suppose the Lord were here now, and you were going to ask Him something—what would you ask Him? We're going to pass this little New Testament around from hand to hand. When it reaches you, you pray. If you don't feel like praying, read a passage. . . . There, that's fine; it will be easier next time. . . . "

The Anglican bishops of London and Southwark sent identical letters to their hundreds of clergymen calling for prayer for the crusade. Other denominational leaders followed suit. Buttons, badges, pennants, and banners were being manufactured by the thousands, all urging the population to pray for London. Special crusade tours were arranged from the United States. I suggested to Billy that we should prepare free church bulletins with blank inside pages for any

Spiritual armor: Team members meet for prayer in a hotel room
on the eve of the month-long Greater London Crusade of 1966.

church that asked for them. The outside pages would carry a message from Billy asking Christians to pray for London. He readily agreed, and thousands of North American churches wrote requesting those bulletin covers.

Looking back, one might wonder why the British people became so involved in the evangelistic efforts of a Baptist preacher from America. Why all the excitement because of a Yank crossing the Big Pond to visit Blighty? But there was a far deeper motive at work. A love confrontation has been going on for centuries between God and Albion, God and the "Scepter'd Isle," God and England, Scotland, and Wales. America has no such ancient tradition. A thousand years ago when that man of God, Alfred the Great, was king of England, it was said that a woman could walk across the island from the Irish Sea to the North Sea without a man laying a finger on her.

In the sixteenth century the Puritan movement became England's Reformation, as the people set about returning their church to the God they knew in Christ. John Richard Green wrote in his *History of the English People*, "No greater moral change ever passed over a nation than passed over England (between 1583 and 1623). England became the people of a book, and that book was the Bible. . . . The whole temper of the nation was changed. A new conception of life and of man superseded the old. A new moral and religious impulse spread through every class. . . . The whole nation became, in fact, a church."[1]

In 1966 the conscience of Britain was beginning once again to show itself. Shades of Bede, of Latimer, of Whitefield, and Wesley! It's as if Billy were the incendiary, as if the British people were calling across the Atlantic and saying, "You are the torch, and we are the heather; set us afire!"

After several days I returned to my desk in Minneapolis, and in late May my wife and I flew back to Heathrow Airport with others of the Graham team. We traveled by train to Southampton to welcome Billy and Ruth and attended his press conference aboard the *H.M.S. Queen Mary*. We then rode the boat train back to Waterloo Station, and that evening we attended a team meeting in a quiet room at our London hotel. Holy Communion was served. Billy told us, "I want with all my heart to lay my life on the line for Jesus Christ. I'm

Youth night: Before the service begins, Billy enjoys repartee with some of London's youth at Earls Court.

not even sure I know how, but I want to." What a thrill just to be there! In each heart excitement was running high. A hush of expectancy came over us as we realized that God's only limitation in London was the limitation we as Christians put on Him.

On the eve of the crusade, the huge Earls Court with its sixteen restaurants was polished spick and span. The ministers and churches were ready.

I cannot possibly recreate for you the atmosphere at the crusade meetings that went on night after night in Earls Court. The music, the preaching, the tears, the smiles, the laughter, the vast crowds, people surging to the altar, the preaching of God's Word, the television cameras, and the singing of old hymns are memories that never seem to die, even though they fade a bit. What I can do best is tell you about some of the curious things that took place during the four weeks.

After one has watched Billy Graham in many different pulpits, it becomes apparent that he never takes charge of a meeting. He always considers himself to be a guest and expects the inviting committee to deal with any unusual behavior among those present.

One evening when Billy had barely started his invitation, a skinny young man with a bad complexion and poorly dressed walked to the front. He stood alone in front of the crowd, looking up and shaking his fist at Billy. Then he turned around to the audience and shouted, "Don't believe it! It's not true. I've tried it!"

Billy immediately stepped back and waited for the host committee to respond. While people prayed for the young man, he was gently escorted out and counseled, and the work of God went on. After all, you can't "try" Christianity. I'm sure someone explained to the young man that only when we stop trying does the grace of God take over our lives.

I remember a similar incident at a meeting in Buenos Aires after Billy had extended an invitation to come to Christ. As people were responding, a robed guest on the platform stood up. He was a bishop of a local Catholic group of churches that were at some variance with the Roman hierarchy. Stepping to the edge of the platform, he began lifting his hands and blessing the people who were walking forward.

A committeeman approached Billy and whispered to him, "You'll have to ask him to stop doing that."

Billy replied, "He's your bishop. You ask him!"

During the London crusade, three American women—Barbara Holmyard, Toni Johnson, and Mildred Dienert—arranged for high teas in one of the Earls Court restaurants and invited society leaders and members of the London aristocracy to come and stay for the services. They came! The women had even provided a dignified announcer who called out the names of the honorable lords and ladies as they made their entrances.

Barbara Holmyard, who had attended one of our writing schools, leaned over to me. "Woody, go over there and come through the entrance, and we'll have you announced." I laughed. Imagine! "Woody Wirt, the Friar of Sherwood Forest," perhaps? But if one of our team should hear that dignified gentleman singing out my name, my goose would have been cooked. My polite refusal may also have been motivated partly by poet Bobby Burns, who wrote:

> Ye see yon birkie [young fellow], ca'd [called] a lord,
>   Wha' struts an' stares an' a' that? . . .
> He's but a cuif [goof] for a' that . . .
>   The man of independent mind,
> He looks and laughs at a' that.[2]

Early in the crusade Dr. Nelson Bell, Billy's father-in-law, sent a worried message by cable from North Carolina to Billy. It seemed the crusade was not attracting much attention in the American press. Some dispatches from London were negative, reporting the audiences below average. The exciting things that were happening at Earls Court, the television breakthrough, the visits to the Soho district, the presence of dignitaries, Billy's visit with the queen, the astonishing youth night services, the vast numbers of inquirers each night were ignored.

I was told Billy wanted to see me in his dressing room at Earls Court. When I got there he was on the telephone to the Associated Press downtown, and the AP was apologizing for the lack of cover-

Team wives: Some of the team members' wives gather outside Spurgeon's Tabernacle on Sunday morning after hearing Ruth Graham speak. London, 1966.

age. The manager was telling Billy that if he could furnish them nightly with crusade news, it would be cabled to America. I heard Billy say, "I'll have a man deliver a story to your office every night at seven o'clock." The AP office apparently thanked him, and Billy put down the phone and left the room.

It seemed everything was settled. No one said anything. Finally I asked Walter Smyth, director of overseas crusades, "Was that me he was talking about?"

"Yes."

"Walter, I'm going home in two days. We've got our tickets. I have a magazine issue to get out."

"You're not going anywhere, Woody. Let Winnie go. You're here for the duration."

A week later Dr. Bell reported that crusade publicity in the American press was picking up.

Much has been written about Billy's visit to the Soho district of London during the crusade. The visit was intended to be a quiet, friendly interchange with the shopkeepers of the rather notorious area, and it ended in a near riot. Billy had made such visits elsewhere. This one, however, was doomed the minute the huge television sound trucks rolled into the area and the crews began rigging up powerful lights. They, more than Billy, were the ones that drew the crowd. Most people had no idea what was going on.

Frustrated by the growing number of spectators in his attempt to visit Soho door to door, Billy, holding a "loud-hailer," jumped on a car and began to address the crowd. At this point a blonde stripper in a miniskirt and little else was lifted up and passed hand-to-hand over the crowd toward him. This was an obvious setup. She reached the car just as Billy jumped down. To get to his own waiting vehicle, Billy had to press through a mob that was becoming increasingly mean. It was push and shove, and his helpers were vastly outnumbered. Something unpleasant was in the air. A fist fight was imminent.

At last Billy's bodyguards reached the corner, slipped him into the car, and slammed the door. Slowly the car pulled away. As it did, the crowd turned around and dispersed as if nothing had happened. In my book it was a close call. God was present.

One evening in Earls Court, Billy had finished preaching and gave his invitation. Nearly a thousand people came forward to commit their lives to Jesus Christ. He was on the platform, praying silently, waiting for the last inquirers to reach the front. The choir had stopped singing. All was serene.

Suddenly a large woman in the front row stood up, threw her head back, and began praying, or perhaps I should say braying, in a loud voice. I had just left my seat at the side and was about to tiptoe around behind the inquirers with a local photographer, looking for an interesting picture or two. Not a person moved toward the vociferous woman, who was actually preventing Billy from speaking. He stepped back and waited. I walked over to her and took her by the arm and in a whisper suggested that we be seated. She threw off my arm and made more noise than ever.

By this time Associate Evangelist Joe Blinco had left the platform and joined me. With the lady in the middle, we gently but firmly walked her down the long center aisle to the end of the Court. She continued screaming, "I plead the blood! I plead the blood!" With all London staring at us, it was the longest walk of my life. Not another sound was heard in the vast arena.

Among the many spiritual gifts I lack is the power to exorcise spirits, but that night I had had enough. Halfway down the aisle, I spotted a policeman standing against the far wall, but he made no move to help us. I turned to the woman and said, "I rebuke you in the name of Jesus Christ and command you to come out of her!"

She continued to shout, but now I heard her saying, "I rebuke you too! I rebuke you too!"

It was my first, last, and only attempt at driving out evil spirits. Joe Blinco and I turned our Cassandra over to the law, while at the other end of the Court, Billy continued undisturbed with his words of inspiration and exhortation to those who had come forward.

Toward the end of the crusade, a call came to the London Billy Graham office from a church in Plymouth, England. They would like a team member to fill their pulpit the coming Sunday. Unfortunately everybody else on the team was already engaged in ministering in churches that day—everybody except Woody. Would he go? He would.

Taking the overnight train, I arrived in Plymouth early on Sunday and was escorted to the church. After preaching from the high pulpit at the rather sparse morning service, I was invited to attend the afternoon youth meeting held in a separate building nearby. There an elaborate "tea" was provided, with plenty of sandwiches for the church's young people and their friends. And there I met the "rockers."

There were four, all wearing badges, gaudily dressed in leather jackets, all long-haired and extremely hungry. I remember two of their names, "Rick" and "Paddy." They ignored my challenge to the young people by remaining outside smoking. Only when it was time to eat did they slip in and gulp down sandwiches as if they were starving.

I was fascinated by these young rebels and tried to dialogue with them. One responded, "You don't want to talk to me, I'm just a sex-crazed maniac." But I did want to talk, and I brought up a subject that interested them.

"Have you heard about Billy Graham?" Yes, they had heard. (Practically everybody in Britain had heard.) So I stuck my neck out—too far out. "Would you like to meet him?" They pricked up their ears. "Next Sunday," I said, "he will be closing the Greater London Crusade in Wembley Stadium. There'll be a huge crowd. But I'll be there, and if you show up, I'll introduce you to Billy. Would you like that?" They thought they would. "Can you get transportation?" They shook their heads. Each one had a motorcycle that had been impounded by the Plymouth police for traffic violations.

"Can you hitch rides? Take a bus?" They might. "I'll see you early Sunday at Wembley."

During the week I had occasion to mention to Billy that some authentic, real-life rockers were coming up from Plymouth for the final meeting at Wembley and were hoping to meet him. Would he like to meet them? He would. On Sunday morning I explained to him that the rockers would be waiting to shake hands with him in the tunnel as he was leaving the stadium that afternoon.

I arrived early at the stadium and found that three of the rockers had arrived after riding all night in a bus. They were already picking a fight with the ushers. It seems the staff was not too interested in admitting these rude young characters. I took them off the ushers' hands and welcomed them. I explained that as Billy's editor, I had access to the press section, and they were to be my guests there. When we got to the press section, we found it empty. No ushers were around. I placed the rockers in the back row of the section and told them to stay there while I went for refreshments.

I returned to find that another fight with the ushers had broken out. The last row of the press section was right in front of the first row of the choir's soprano section, which was already overflowing with charming ladies. They indignantly resented the noisy youths sprawled in front of them.

It took all my brass to insist again to the ushers and all concerned that these three young men were special guests of the team and that I had "every right as Billy's editor" to put them in the press section. Finally they were left alone, and they sat with me through the service, along with 94,344 others in that packed stadium.

Rockers vs. the usher: Three rockers, who came to hear Billy Graham at Wembley Stadium, tangle with an usher. Two of them gave their lives to Christ.

The songs were sung, the Gospel was preached, and when the invitation was given, I beckoned them to follow me. We slipped quietly down to the secret tunnel that allows Wembley Stadium special guests to make a quick exit to the parking lot. In the middle of the rather lengthy tunnel, I stopped and asked the fellows to stand against the wall. Visibility was not the best, but I noticed that only two of them were with me. After several minutes we heard voices, and a large body of men came thundering through the tunnel. I stepped out squarely in front of them, and they looked as if they were going to run me down. However, I caught Billy's eye and pointed to the two young men standing against the wall.

"Oh!" he said with a sudden smile. He stepped over and shook hands quickly. The entourage went on, and I praised the Lord. The great crusade was over. I had kept my promise made in Plymouth, and the rockers had come to Wembley and met Billy Graham.

All except the third rocker. He had gone forward with nearly 4,000 other inquirers. He did not meet Billy. He met Jesus. And, as I learned later, so did one of the other two.

Dear, Mr Graham.

I was just wacthing your shaw and I reard you say to mi write you for a pamphlete. So I went in to the bath tub and while I was in there I remmbered what you said. So I ask the lord to come into my hart. And then I got out of the tube and said mum can I write to you.

GOD·BLESS YOU,

Yours
turly.
David Osborne
age 10.

Surrey B.C.

Seventeen

WITH THE TROOPS
IN VIETNAM

~

WE WILL REJOICE IN YOUR SALVATION, AND IN THE NAME
OF OUR GOD WE WILL SET UP OUR BANNERS!

—PSALM 20:5

B illy Graham had hoped to join the Army Chaplain Corps during World War II, but he was prevented by illness from completing his application. To be candid, I have never known anyone
who worked harder at being a chaplain than Billy did while he was
in Vietnam. In fact, ministering to and encouraging chaplains was a
major element in his two Christmas visits to the Southeast Asia war
zone in 1966 and 1968.

My own tour of duty as an Army Air Corps chaplain took me to
the Aleutian Islands. Billy Graham's voluntary tour of duty took him
into the very heart of the combat areas of Vietnam. He went as a volunteer seeking to bring spiritual strength and encouragement to the
troops, at the invitation of General William C. Westmoreland, commanding general of the American forces. Billy was accompanied in
1966 by four of his team members, song leader Cliff Barrows, soloist
George Beverly Shea, pianist Tedd Smith, and the late Dan Piatt, tour
manager.

The following description is based on reports written at my
request by Tedd Smith, which I published in *Decision* magazine at
the time.[1] The team toured field hospitals, servicemen's centers,
Vietnamese villages, mess halls, officers' clubs, improvised chapels,

and schools built by American servicemen for Vietnamese children. Billy also spoke to large groups of chaplains, not only those under American colors, but also to chaplains from Australia and New Zealand, who were equally committed to the war effort.

Refusing to stay in the safer Saigon area with the touring entertainers, Billy insisted on going north toward the DMZ (demilitarized zone) located on the seventeenth parallel between North and South Vietnam. At An Khe the troops stood in boot-top mud and held 4,000 burning candles at a Christmas Eve candlelight service led by Billy. In Nha Trang he hosted a fellowship dinner for missionaries and chaplains and Vietnamese pastors. Rev. Doan Van Mieng (who was later arrested and sent to a Communist prison) invited Billy to return to Vietnam to hold an evangelistic crusade. Billy and the team also took helicopter tours to visit schools and dedicate chapels.

Billy's object was not primarily to fulfill a duty or leave an impression. *He was after souls*. The very intensity of his ministry as he presented the Gospel to the troops—urging them to make a lifetime response—revealed his life-and-death concern for the men facing death daily amid all the horrors of the battlefield.

Candlelight services were held after dark, and at each stop the men were challenged to commit their lives to Jesus Christ. At Long Binh Cliff Barrows led 6,000 people in singing Christmas carols. At Hammond Air Base it rained, but a Sky Trooper joined Billy to help bring the Christmas spirit to the men. On Christmas Day Billy preached to 5,000 marines in the Freedom Hill Amphitheatre in the port city of DaNang, close to the combat zone.

The headquarters staff chaplain, Col. Walter Sugg, summed it up: "The Billy Graham team's ministry was warmly received, and the response was an inspiration. Hundreds and thousands of men came in brilliant sun, steaming heat, rain, and mud. Their reluctance to depart following each service evidenced the depths the message had reached."

Two years later Billy made a second Christmas visit to Vietnam. This time his team consisted of Associate Evangelist T. W. Wilson, soloist Jimmie McDonald, and again pianist Tedd Smith. A Hong Kong newspaper, the *South China Morning Post*, stated on their arrival in Saigon, "Billy Graham will give the troops, irrespective of color or creed, some comfort at Christmas and perhaps the kind of peace that can never be found around a political conference table."

The team then flew further north to Phu Bai, where they were welcomed by a war hero, Gen. Richard G. Stilwell. Five thousand troops assembled in pouring rain in Camp Hochmuth Amphitheatre to hear Billy introduce his message with the words: "I come to bring you greetings from millions of Americans who are proud of you and what you are doing."

That afternoon the team visited a naval hospital ship, and the service was broadcast over the ship's television to all the wards. The visitors were then taken by COD aircraft to the carrier *USS Ranger*, where a Christmas service was conducted in the ship's hangar for 2,700 men. Several destroyers pulled alongside the *Ranger* so their troops could share the service by closed-circuit television.

Another great Christmas service was held on December 23 at Danang, this time complete with marine band and choir. The marines walked in from a fifteen-mile radius and waited for hours for the worship to begin. At Billy's invitation, hundreds raised their hands to receive Jesus Christ as Savior and Lord.

On Christmas Day, 1968, the team was back in Saigon holding two morning services at the Tan Son Nhut air base. The second service was broadcast to every American Armed Services station throughout the world and was carried in the United States on the Mutual network. The team spent the afternoon visiting fire support bases in three areas of intense fighting.

As they prepared to return home the next day, Tedd Smith wrote:

It is difficult for me personally to summarize such a meaningful time with our troops. To visit hospitals where men lie with both legs amputated and who are yet able to smile and say, "There's a reason for this . . . Merry Christmas;" to visit wards on hospital ships and derive strength and confidence from the dedicated doctors and nurses; to talk with fighter pilots who face danger every single mission they fly; to speak with a man on the front lines facing the Viet Cong night by night, knowing he's got to stay on for another eleven months; to learn something of the splendid work of the chaplaincy; to talk to volunteer workers of the USO and Red Cross; to see thousands of pieces of mail and gift packages arriving from America addressed to unknown soldiers and sent just to say, "Thank you—we're praying for you"; to see a nineteen-year-old soldier weeping openly and throwing his arms around you and saying, "I found God today, sir. I really did"; just to have had the privilege of going to Vietnam and saying, "God bless you, and Merry Christmas"—how can one describe the impact of such an experience? And it was all to present the One whom Christmas is all about.

So close to my heart is this story that I have saved it until the last. Before the 1966 Christmas visit of Billy to Vietnam, team member Dan Piatt went to Saigon and visited Gen. William Westmoreland to complete the itinerary and finalize arrangements. The general then asked, "Is there anything more we can do for you, Dan?"

"Well, sir," said Dan, "there's a marine lance corporal serving up there near the DMZ who is the son of one of our team members. It would be very special if he could be allowed to come to hear Mr. Graham in DaNang."

"No problem, Dan."

So at Christmastime a marine helicopter was dispatched to a point near the DMZ to pick up a somewhat bewildered lance corporal named Alexander Wirt. When he arrived in DaNang, he was ordered to be at ease, eat three meals a day, and wait. This young man, who happens to be my son, had worked at wrapping packages a year earlier in the basement of the Billy Graham Association head offices in Minneapolis, Minnesota.

Three days later Billy flew into DaNang, and on Christmas Day Lance Corporal Wirt learned why he was there. He joined 5,000 other marines listening to the Gospel in Freedom Hill Amphitheatre. After the service ended, Wirt went to the front of the speaker's platform where other marines had gathered for Billy's autograph on their Bibles and fliers.

The speaker patted his shirt apologetically and said, "I don't believe I have a pen with me."

At this point Alexander spoke up. "Here's a pen, sir. You can keep it; it belongs to you anyway."

A Bible verse was inscribed on the pen.

Billy smiled, leaned over, and took a closer look at the marine. "You must be Woody Wirt's son!" he exclaimed.

"Yes, sir." They shook hands and talked for a while.

The helicopter later returned the lance corporal to a new post of duty with the Marine Corps pacification program. Before he left, Tedd Smith obtained from him a quote that appeared in the March 1967 issue of *Decision:* "Said Lance Corporal Alexander W. Wirt of Minnesota, U.S. Marines, 3rd Division (CAC), who attended the great service of worship in DaNang on Christmas Day, 'It was wonderful to see the team again. It was like coming home.'"

In a letter to his parents, Alex wrote that the team visit reminded him of why he was there and of all the people at home who were praying for him.

Dear Mr. Graham,

Will you tell god to forgive
what I done all these years.
I am in the third grade
and I am eight years old.
Is it too late for me to
be forgived by god?

Francis Johnson Hill

Eighteen

WAR AND PEACE
IN KOREA

~

THE LORD OF HOSTS IS WITH US;
THE GOD OF JACOB IS OUR REFUGE.

—PSALM 46:11

Billy Graham's introduction to Korea in 1952 came as a result of the written appeals of American military chaplains whose troops were finally engaged in combat with Communists in what President Harry Truman described as a "United Nations Peace Action."

Wheels turned, and in December 1952, as guest of the Pentagon and Supreme Allied Commander General Mark Clark, Billy toured the hospitals and MASH (Mobile Army Surgical Hospital) units of South Korea. Grady Wilson and Bob Pierce, founder of World Vision, accompanied him as they visited the tragic victims of the "peace action."

It was Billy's first exposure to the grisly realities of modern warfare. He prayed with men without eyes and limbs, with gaping wounds and charred skin. In his book *Count It All Joy*, Grady Wilson has left us an account of one unforgettable scene:

> They had helicoptered in a young soldier who had been machine-gunned in the back. He was permanently paralyzed and was lying facedown on a canvas rigging in a MASH unit of the Tenth Corps. Billy had spoken briefly over a PA system, and when he stopped by this patient, he heard him say gasping, "Mr. Graham, I heard your message. I want to tell you

that even though I can't move, it's worth being machine-gunned to open my heart to Jesus Christ. This day I have accepted Jesus Christ as my Savior."

Then the soldier added, "Mr. Graham, I would like to see your face."

Billy obligingly got down and lay on his back alongside so the young man could have eye contact with him. A tear fell on Billy's face. Billy also was fighting tears as he softly talked and prayed with a young man whom he will one day meet again.

It was Christmas Eve.[1]

Coming into South Korea two decades later in the spring of 1973, we found it all so different. Seoul, the capital, was now a beautiful rebuilt city. It seemed to many of us on the Billy Graham team that we were coming into God's country. We found Christians rising at 4 A.M. and going to an hour's service of holy worship in a church before leaving for their workplace. In Seoul we found the largest Presbyterian church in the whole world, the largest Methodist church in the world, and the largest Assemblies of God church in the world, with over a million members. Here also we found a love for the Lord Jesus Christ that reminded us of the way the people of Asia received the Gospel from the apostle Paul and his teammates in New Testament times.

After months of preaching efforts by his team in all of South Korea's major cities, Billy spent a week proclaiming Christ to hundreds of thousands of Koreans on Yo-ido Plaza outside Seoul. The amazing climax came on Sunday afternoon, June 3, when Billy addressed 1,100,000 people who had come (mostly on foot) to the Plaza. He told the vast assemblage, "This has been the greatest experience of my life."

Billy also did something for which I have always honored him. It was a small thing really. Before the service began, much to our surprise, Billy invited each member of his team to step up to the platform and be photographed next to him with that record-breaking crowd in the background.

Such a minor happening hardly needs to be mentioned, you

Great day in Korea: More than 1,100,000 people gather in Seoul, South Korea, for the closing Sunday service in the 1973 crusade. Billy stands with his editor.

might say. Yet that is precisely why I mention it. Naturally we were charmed. I look at that picture of Billy and myself every day. It reminds me of Grady Wilson's war story because it tells me of what quality stuff Billy Graham is made.

When the crusade opened on Yo-ido Island, the American ambassador was present. So was Dr. Kyung Chik Han, the great Christian statesman and pastor emeritus of Young Nak Church in Seoul. So was Dr. Paul Yonggi Cho, pastor of the world's largest church in Seoul. So were 11,000 trained counselors, 3,608 pastors, and an audience half a mile long. All those people were ready and eager seemingly for Billy to show them how to enter the kingdom of

God. All the program formalities and the protocol of a public event in a foreign country were about to begin.

For weeks all of us on the team had labored hard on Korean soil, and the response to the gospel message was fabulous. In Pusan Grady Wilson preached to 326,000 people, including 60,000 school children on a Saturday afternoon. In Chonju Howard Jones preached to 270,000 and spoke by invitation at a Buddhist seminary. In Taejon Akbar Abdul-Haqq spoke to 83,500. John Wesley White spoke to 140,000 in Taegu. Cliff Barrows spoke to 37,000 in Choon Chun. Ralph Bell spoke to 320,000 in a ball park in Kwangju. Other members of the team included musicians George Beverly Shea, Tedd Smith, John Innes, Henry Holley (the crusade director, who in the nineties is still ministering in Korea), Don Bailey, Lee Fisher, Steve Musto, Ted Cornell, Bill Fasig, Tom Bledsoe, Randall Veazey, and even myself.

I was escorted to Inchon one day to evangelize the Republic of Korea troops and to enjoy tea with His Excellency, the general. What an honor to preach Christ to those men through an interpreter! I remember it well because after I spoke, a senior officer loudly reprimanded the ROK chaplains then busily circulating among those who had come down front at the invitation. The chaplains were getting names and serial numbers for their spiritual follow-up!

The evangelist's wife, Ruth Bell Graham, was also present and addressed thousands of women in a meeting at Seoul's Ewha University. As a thirteen-year-old daughter of missionary parents, Ruth Bell had attended a Christian high school in Pyongyang, capital of North Korea. At the time of our crusade in 1973, the Pyongyang Communist government conducted a campaign of vilification against her husband, calling him "the sorcerer from America" who had come to South Korea to "practice fanatic exorcism and spread superstition."[2] More recently, however, Dr. and Mrs. Graham have been invited guests of the government in Pyongyang and have been graciously treated. As a gesture of love, the Grahams have donated a clinic-on-wheels for treating the children of North Korea.

One of my unforgettable recollections was on Friday evening at the Plaza when the worship leaders invited the people to pray. Can

Reunion: Ruth Graham and the editor with his World Vision-sponsored "daughter," Choon Hee, at a team reception.

you imagine the sound of 600,000 voices all offering different prayers to God at the same time? It was incredible, and yet I'm sure they were all duly noted in heaven.

Yes, to us who were there in Korea in 1973, the crusade is a wonderful memory. For myself something special was added. My late wife, Winola, and I for many years had supported a Korean orphan under the World Vision program started by founder Bob Pierce. When I arrived in Seoul, the World Vision representatives brought my sponsored "daughter," Choon Hee, from her coastal home, where she was a kindergarten teacher, to visit me. So for four brief, joyful days of my life, I had a daughter of my own. Of course it was Korea, and we could only communicate by signs and interpreters, and we have lost touch since, but still—four days!

Someday beyond the sunset we will speak the same language.

Nineteen

MIRACLE IN JOHANNESBURG

~

GO HOME TO YOUR FRIENDS, AND TELL THEM WHAT
GREAT THINGS THE LORD HAS DONE FOR YOU.

—MARK 5:19

They came on foot in the hot autumn sunshine. They came leaning on sticks and riding in wheelchairs, on scooters, motorbikes,
Austin-Healeys, Mercedes, green buses (for blacks) and red buses (for
whites). They came by black train and white train; by chartered bus
from East London, Pretoria, Port Elizabeth, Bloemfontein,
Ladysmith, Newcastle, Queenstown, and Salisbury; by jet from
Durban and Cape Town.

They came from the carefully controlled "native" suburbs that
fanned out from Jo'burg; from Soweto, Sharpeville, Naledi,
Moletsane, Phirio, Dube, Phefeni, Phomolong, and Meadowlands;
from the "Indian" city of Lenasia and the "coloured" (or mixed)
cities of Kliptown and Noordgesig.

They came by motorcar from the pleasant "European" suburbs
of the great city, as well as from towns along the fabled
Witwatersrand, the "ridge of the white waters"—from Nigel,
Brakpan, Gedult, Benoni, Boksburg, Alberton, Edenvale, Germiston,
Roodepoort, Krugersdorp, and Randfontein. They came from urban
high-rises and luxury hotels and from kraals in the rural veldt.

They came wearing pith helmets and walrus mustaches; colorful
Jesus jerseys and Oxford "bags"; sports blazers, safari suits, and

leopard-skin hats; black lace doilies and shocking pink doeks; purple stocks of the cloth, African beads, and goatskin sashes. They carried parasols and picnic lunches and made shade hats out of the Sunday *Express*.

They came from tribal churches of the Zulu, Xhosa, Tswana, Shangaan, Swazi, Sotho, Ndbele, Venda, Tsonga, and Bapedi people; they came from white Afrikaner churches, white and "coloured" English churches, Chinese churches, black churches, Indian churches, gospel chapels, and Jesus groups.

Into Johannesburg they came, or "eGoli" as the Zulus call it, the "golden city on the reefs," bringing their history with them and making history as they came. They sat on the grass, leaned out windows, perched on rooftops, and clambered up the sides of the scoreboards. And why had they come? To hear the man preach the Gospel of Jesus Christ. To learn the way of God's salvation and, in the case of thousands, to respond with a life commitment.[1]

This was Sunday afternoon, March 25, 1973, in Wanderers Cricket Ground in the prosperous capital city of the gold-rich Transvaal. It had taken the Christians of South Africa twenty-six years of repeated invitations before Billy Graham consented to come to their land, and then only if they promised that the meetings would be racially integrated.

Subdued excitement pervaded the record-breaking crowd of 60,000 persons. Special music was provided by the Power and Light Revolution, a Youth for Christ singing ensemble, and by four young Zulu men who made up the Gospel Truth Quartet. The service was carried to the largest radio audience in the history of South Africa, both in English and in Afrikaans.

The sermon was on a familiar text, John 3:16 (KJV): "For God so loved the world that he gave his only begotten Son, that whosoever believeth in him should not perish, but have everlasting life." In the message that followed, Mr. Graham said, "Every secret thing you've ever done will one day be flashed on the scoreboards of heaven. . . . My wife says that marriage is a union of two good forgivers. . . . You in South Africa are going to have to learn to be for-

Goodbye, apartheid: At a 1973 Sunday rally in Johannesburg's Wanderers Cricket Ground, the South African races come together for the first time in a mass gesture of Christian love as Billy preaches the Gospel.

givers. . . . We are one in Christ! . . . South Africa can no longer live in isolation from the rest of the world."

He then invited the people to repent, accept God's forgiveness, and receive new life in Jesus Christ. A grassy perimeter of 100 feet around the platform had been kept clear for inquirers. At this appeal came an unforgettable sight. Thousands of people of all races moved out of the stands, picking their way past the folks seated on the grass. Hundreds never got near the platform but stood in improvised aisles, quietly, with bowed heads.

After repeating the prayer of commitment, the inquirers were counseled in eleven different languages and dialects by 2,000 Christian volunteers. Watching it, one got the impression that Johannesburg would never again be quite the same. As Anglican Bishop Alphaeus Zulu of Zululand expressed it to me: "The sight of black and white South Africa together in that field, singing and praying to the one God, was a foretaste of what future generations in this land are certain to enjoy if we today will be faithful."

One of the black members of the Billy Graham team, Dr. Howard O. Jones, observed:

> For many (black) Christians it was their first glimpse of a brother from America with a skin color other than white. Just my presence seemed to give them hope. As they confided in me, there was much praying and sharing.
>
> Today South Africa stands at the crossroads. It was the feeling of all, white and black Christians alike, that change will come. It is our prayer that this change will come through the reconciliation of man with man at the cross of Jesus Christ.

What men and women could only hope for that day at Wanderers Cricket Ground is now reality. South Africa is a united nation under black leadership, and it came about peaceably by God's grace. Those of us who were there in 1973 can look back now and say that it was a wonderful and glorious experience. Through a man's faithful ministry, almighty God gave the promise of something permanent, and in time it actually came to pass.

And where was I in all this? I was up on the rim of the stadium, walking around and laughing as I watched people gingerly approaching the toilet houses, each painted white (for use by "whites") and yellow (for "coloureds"). At each toilet house around the stadium rim, men wearing white shirts and badges were standing by the entrances smiling, waving, and shouting, "It's all right. Anybody can use them. Come in, they're open to everybody!"

Think of it. All this and heaven too!

Twenty

ALASKA:
TWO MEN PRAYED

~

IF TWO OF YOU AGREE ON EARTH CONCERNING ANYTHING THAT
THEY ASK, IT WILL BE DONE FOR THEM BY MY FATHER IN HEAVEN.

—MATTHEW 18:19

The story of the Anchorage crusade really begins in the eighteenth and nineteenth centuries when the first Christian missionaries arrived in Alaska. Innokenti Veniaminoff, a Siberian priest of the Russian Orthodox faith, pioneered God's work among the Aleutian peoples. He built churches that are still active, for there are Orthodox congregations all along the southern coast of Alaska. He was an excellent man, memorialized in the hearts of Alaskans and by a snow-capped volcanic peak of 8,200 feet named for him in the Aleutian Range.

After him came Sheldon Jackson, a Presbyterian missionary and another great man. He brought in reindeer to augment the diet of impoverished Eskimos. Then came S. Hall Young to Juneau and Father Duncan to Metlakatla and Archdeacon Hudson Stuck to Fort Yukon and the Moravians to Bethel. But missionary work in Alaska has always been hard, and the results were meager.

I was no missionary, but a godless, threadbare news reporter when I arrived in Alaska on a steerage ticket aboard the *S.S. Alaska* in October 1935. I was twenty-four, and my worldly wealth consisted of twelve dollars, but, lo and behold, a newspaper job in Juneau turned up and became my meal ticket for four years.

I remember once asking Father Kashevaroff, curator of the Territorial Museum, what the Eskimo people thought of God. He said the Eskimos had no notion of God. They only knew demons, whom they feared and sought to appease. Once on a rowboat trip down the Yukon River I found baby boots tied to the paling of an Indian grave on the riverbank, evidently for a memorial to this world and a gift for the next.

This was Alaska. Small churches, small interest, small vision, but a great and mighty land, rich beyond human imagination.

Billy Graham had some interest in Alaska. Once en route to the 1967 Tokyo crusade, he had stopped in Anchorage and talked with Christian people at the airport. At the time nothing further developed, but he did not forget.

On November 7, 1978, Billy reached his sixtieth birthday. I had conceived the idea of a *festschrift* of essays to be written by his friends and presented to the evangelist on that festive day. His family approved, and the response from Billy's friends was enthusiastic, so I spent several months of retirement editing and putting the book together.

Word Publishers released it in an attractive volume under the title *Evangelism: The Next Ten Years*, with the subtitle *Essays Presented to Dr. Billy Graham*.[1] Among the contributors were Archbishop Marcus Loane, Primate of Australia; Bishop Maurice Wood of Norwich, England; Dr. Philip Teng of Hong Kong; Dr. Harold Ockenga; Dr. Oswald Hoffmann; Rev. Tom Houston; Evangelists Leighton Ford and Luis Palau, and others.

In November I flew to Charlotte, North Carolina, for the birthday presentation. It was made by Floyd Thatcher of Word Books from the pulpit of a church where Billy was preaching. Afterward a few of us were invited to a private home for the birthday party. There I found myself seated on a sofa and chatting with Billy. The moment was auspicious for the introducing of a subject that had nothing to do with the book.

"Billy," I said, "there is one place you haven't been that needs you badly, and that's Alaska."

His response was immediate. "I'd like to go to Alaska. You used to live there, didn't you? . . . "

It did not take me long to notify Dr. Sterling Huston, director of North American crusades, of Billy's response. Sterling had already received overtures written on sealskin from Christians in Alaska. But Sterling's desk was piled high with other requests and invitations addressed to Billy from every point of the compass. In addition, he was heavily involved in preparations for actual North American crusades and rallies in Nova Scotia, Wisconsin, Indiana, Alberta, Nevada, and Florida. Alaska must have seemed to Sterling a long way off.

A few weeks later I was back in Alaska, not for Billy this time, but as an invited guest of the Central Alaska Mission. Using a small plane that landed on paved highways, we toured and ministered to Christian groups in such exciting places as Eagle, Dawson, Fairbanks, Tok, Glennallen, and other settlements. Our mission ended in Anchorage. There, while making plans for a writers' seminar sponsored by Alaska Bible College, I renewed friendship with a local minister, Dr. Thomas Teply. He had been my pastor in Minneapolis and was now pastor of Anchorage's First Presbyterian Church. I also met his friend, Rev. Victor Zacharias, who pastored a fine Conservative Baptist church.

Knowing something of Billy's ways, I suggested to these two men of God that they start praying together regularly and asking God to bring a Billy Graham crusade to Alaska to proclaim the Gospel to the people of the forty-ninth state.

Back in the 1930s when I was a young reporter in Juneau, the Territory of Alaska's population had been 60,000, divided about equally between "natives" and "whites." Now Anchorage alone had a population of 200,000. The state was number one in sad statistics, such as alcoholism and suicide percentages, and lowest in church attendance. The vastness of the north country, the climate, crowded towns, and attendant disadvantages created enormous social problems.

I left Anchorage after two days for San Diego and home, but Tom and Vic took my challenge to heart. If Billy wanted to come to

Alaska, they wanted him. On Wednesday noon, November 22, 1978, the two men held their first weekly sack-lunch prayer meeting. According to Tom, "At first we were simply praying for an answer. Was this a proper request? It seemed to us there were so many immediate matters that needed help from God. But after many months of earnest prayer, sometimes with others, usually alone, we both believed that God would be pleased to have us pray definitely for a crusade, so we shifted our emphasis."

In March 1979, the two pastors invited 169 churches and Christian organizations in the Anchorage area to a complimentary luncheon at the First Presbyterian Church on May 2. Eighty-six ministers agreed to come, and fifty-one actually attended. It was agreed at the meeting that they would write to Sterling Huston as director of North American crusades for Billy Graham and invite him to visit their city.

Sterling is one of the world's most gracious and tactful persons,

Under Northern Lights: Sourdoughs, natives, and cheechakos (newcomers) flew in from the Arctic, the Aleutians, and all over Alaska to fill the George L. Sullivan Arena in Anchorage for the Graham crusade in March 1984.

but in 1979 his work calendar was extremely full. Even so the overture from Alaska was properly acknowledged, and the lines of communication were kept open. The prayer meetings of Tom and Vic continued week by week. A year passed, and things began to move. In September 1980, Sterling Huston flew north and met with twenty concerned Christians at breakfast and 120 more at lunch. He thanked the Alaskans for their invitation and reassured them about Dr. Graham's interest in coming there. He also gave them suggestions as to how to prepare spiritually.

An executive committee for the proposed crusade was formed with Henry Pratt as chairman and Richard Anglemyer as treasurer. The original two-man prayer team kept praying.

In May and October 1981, Sterling returned to Anchorage, and hope for a crusade took a great leap forward. On Wednesday, May 19, 1982, Sterling asked me to fly up there to speak at a prayer rally. The aim was to build spiritual momentum among the members of the supporting churches. I was to urge the church folk to join the executive committee and the prayer warriors, Tom and Vic (who were still meeting and still praying), in seeking God's gracious help.

When I arrived for the rally, I learned that Sterling had won the full cooperation of the archbishop of the Anchorage diocese, Francis T. Hurley, who promised to urge all Roman Catholics to attend as many crusade meetings as they could—a remarkable spiritual breakthrough. We had a well-attended prayer rally in the Presbyterian church with lots of intercession and singing, and the two daily newspapers began to show interest.

After I left, the two-man prayer team kept on, with help. A tentative date was set to hold the crusade in 1983, but construction delays on the new 9,000-seat George L. Sullivan Arena caused further postponements. It was not until March 11, 1984, that Billy Graham and his team finally arrived in Anchorage to open the Alaska crusade.

Alaska was more than ready for them. The response was beyond all expectations. To help my memory, I am drawing on *Decision* editor Roger Palms's fine account of what happened in Anchorage. It is full of gripping stories of people who made commitments to Christ.

One jogger who was running past the arena at about 5 P.M. stopped a counselor and asked if he was connected with the crusade. Told that he was, the jogger stood in the middle of the street and said he wanted to change his life and turn to God.

People flew in from the oil rigs, mining camps, and fishing boats. They came from Barrow at the "top of the world," from Prudhoe Bay, from Nome and Point Hope and Kodiak Island and Juneau and Ketchikan. *Cheechakos* (newcomers), sourdoughs (old-timers), natives (Indians and Eskimos) all joined the crowds that for eight nights filled the arena to hear the Gospel.

Walter Maillelle, chairman of the Native Committee for the crusade, said, "This is the greatest thing that has ever happened in Alaska. Every night I see native people coming forward." At least two Russian Orthodox men made new commitments to Christ (Bishop Veniaminoff in heaven must have been smiling.) And each night buses rolled into the arena parking lot from nearby Elmendorf Air Force Base, where I once served as a chaplain.

A School of Evangelism for ministers drew 500 pastors and church leaders. Counseling of inquirers was carried on in Thai, Russian, and Aleut languages as well as English. The Koreans present translated every service into their own language and reaped fruit among their people.

Billy had kindly invited me to come to Anchorage for the crusade. My wife, Winola, was under a doctor's care, but I managed to fly north on Tuesday, March 13, and attended two meetings at the Sullivan Arena. How glorious to see and hear 9,000 Alaskans—think of it!—under one roof singing praises to God for His Son Jesus Christ. And to see them go forward at the invitation in large numbers to receive Christ!

What fun it was to be again with the team and with my Alaskan friends. What a wonderful feeling to shake hands with Billy and to thank him for coming, just as three of us weak-kneed mortals—Tom, Vic and Woody—had hoped and prayed he would, nearly six years before!

For Billy it was not an easy week. He squeezed his days in Alaska into an overcrowded schedule. Then he developed laryngitis so acutely that on Thursday evening he suddenly stopped in the middle of a sermon based on Samson and Delilah and said, "My voice is gone." He turned around on the platform and went back to his seat. Immediately Associate Evangelist John Wesley White, who had been sitting near him, stepped to the pulpit and finished the sermon brilliantly, if extemporaneously.

When John gave the invitation at the close to come to Christ, Billy rose from his seat and without speaking, held out his arms and beckoned the people to come forward. They came! It was a biblical moment. Statistics later showed that the 486 inquirers who went forward in commitment that night were the highest percentage relative to attendance of the entire week. The Sullivan Arena attendance count that evening was 8,700.

The outreach of the Anchorage crusade was fabulous. Ninety percent of the state of Alaska was covered by television rebroadcasts of the meetings. The gospel outreach went by radio over the North Pole to Siberia, Finland, and to a 9,500-mile radius over the Pacific, expanding out of Billy's radio station, KAIM, in Honolulu. In Seoul, South Korea, one congregation met for an hour every morning that week to pray for the crusade.

But the one precious moment I shall always carry with me occurred on Tuesday evening just as I arrived breathlessly from the Anchorage airport. I entered the jam-packed arena as the crusade service was about to begin and was escorted quickly down the aisle toward the platform. Suddenly someone slipped out of one of the aisles and grasped me. It was Tom Teply, and his face was shining. "Woody, do you remember," he asked, "when we started praying for this way back when? Do you remember? And God did it. Wow!"

We hugged and laughed, and I continued walking until another man came out of his seat and accosted me. This time it was Vic Zacharias. He too seized my hand and then hugged me and said, "God heard us, Woody. All those months and years of praying. Nobody knew about it—only a few—and this came out of it. Can you believe it? Look at this crowd. Praise the Lord!"

The usher who had been waiting now escorted me to the platform. I took a back seat, smiled at Billy, Grady, T. W., Tedd, and others on the team, looked at the dazzling crowd—and eight years dropped away. The choir rose for the opening hymn, and there was glory all around.

THE
RIPE
GRAIN

~

Ron Wary
Aristes P.A. 17920
July 18 1913

Dear Billy

I have earned this money picking strawberrys.
So I want to give this money to help some one.
My Grandmother gave me the envlope to send to you.
She said when you give the Lord 1/10 of you earned
He will provide you with another job
or another way to make money for the Lord

Your strawberry picker
Ron Wary

Twenty-One

LEADERSHIP

~

WHOEVER DESIRES TO BECOME GREAT AMONG YOU
SHALL BE YOUR SERVANT.

—MARK 10:43

We hear them everywhere—people crying out for worthy, inspiring leadership. They freely acknowledge the dearth of it. In a time of stress such as ours, people in business, politics, the military, and even education are increasingly citing a religious personality, Billy Graham, not only as a living American legend but as one of the world's outstanding leaders.

Yet this man, as I have indicated, commands no armies, rules no industrial empires, and makes no claim to political influence. How can he be so widely honored as one of the most respected figures of the twentieth century? Why, in a day of antiheroes, has he become a hero? What brought it all about?

The world has its explanations.

"Cream rises to the top."

"Deserve success, and you shall command it."

But the Bible has a different answer. It says that when a man's ways please the Lord, He makes even his enemies to be at peace with him.[1] And Billy Graham reads his Bible.

Millions of young men and women are starting out in life today with an intense desire to be leaders. They are pumping iron, taking seminars, joining groups, reading books, and watching films that depict strong, domineering, even brutal men and women who battle their way to mighty achievements. Oh, to be on top! Oh, to command!

Jesus, the greatest leader of mankind in history, had an answer for all such seekers. You will find it in the New Testament, in the tenth chapter of the Gospel of Mark. This passage relates that two of Jesus' disciples, James and John, went to Jesus and asked Him for positions of leadership. They said to Him, "Grant us that we may sit, one on Your right hand and the other on Your left, in Your glory."[2]

That is, of course, precisely the worst way to go about becoming a leader. Jesus knew what the sons of Zebedee were really looking for. It was power—power as authority and power as sheer strength. He also knew that their request would certainly create dissension among His other disciples. He wasted no time in answering to the effect: "I'm sorry, men, it's not My department."[3]

Then summoning the rest of the disciples, Jesus set forth for all time His divine criteria for true leadership (Mark 10:35-41). The rules are quite simple. Jesus said that in the world the "great ones" exercise authority and lordship ("lord it over") other people. Then He added, "It shall not be so among you; but whoever desires to become great among you shall be your servant. And whoever of you desires to be first shall be slave of all."

Jesus not only talked about leadership, but He also set His men an example. At the Last Supper He girded himself with a towel and washed the disciples' feet—obviously the role of a menial servant. Then after the Resurrection, when His disciples had returned to Galilee and had gone fishing, He quietly appeared on the scene and cooked breakfast for them.

Such activities are not listed in any textbooks on leadership that I know of, but they are found in the Bible. What do they tell us about Jesus as a leader? They show that He loved His team, enjoyed fellowship with them, and would do almost anything for them. In no way did He consciously elevate Himself above His men in a physical sense. He was no demagogue. On the contrary, He went out of His way to show willingness to serve His friends. The result was an amazing upsurge of loyalty among the eleven disciples. Remember, these eleven were not always models of support toward Jesus. They doubted Him, denied Him, and left Him; but He bountifully forgave them. The temple guard told the truth when he said, "No man ever spoke like this Man!"[4]

At times when Jesus was teaching, His words must have had an unforgettable ring. Matthew wrote, "The people were astonished at His teaching, for He taught them as one having authority, and not as the scribes."[5] Matthew was describing his Leader in action.

Far be it from me to compare Billy Graham (or anyone else) to his Master, but I wish I could describe to you how Billy Graham preached the Gospel when he was in his thirties and forties and fifties. A biographer, William Martin, wrote of "the clenched fist, the pointing finger, the ambidextrous slashes, the two-pistol punctuation, the riveting effect." Stenographers have reportedly estimated that he spoke 240 words a minute.[6] Yet the foregoing description utterly fails to capture his passionate sincerity.

Those of us who heard him then remember the mind-boggling way he proclaimed the Gospel. His air of authority seemed invincible. From the day he started to preach, Billy Graham said what he meant and meant what he said. He talked, and still talks, about repentance for sin and godly sorrow. He talks about the blood of Christ, shed by our Savior to make atonement for our sins. He talks about Jesus Christ risen from the dead, about the Holy Spirit, and about the return of Christ in glory. He doesn't mince words or qualify meaning. John Stott, chaplain to Her Majesty the Queen, states it better than I can: "There isn't an iota of hypocrisy in the man. He is real. I sat in Harringay [Arena] night after night asking over and over, 'What is the reason?' I finally decided that this was the first time most of these people had heard a transparently honest evangelist who was speaking from his heart and who meant and believed what he was saying."[7]

Let me tell you some stories about Billy Graham that bring out different aspects of his leadership.

In the summer of 1967 I was with Billy during his crusade in Winnipeg, Manitoba. During that week our team attended a dinner party that had been arranged in a hotel for a large number of Billy's

Canadian friends and supporters. We all sat at small tables, a team member at each one. During the meal Billy came around to each table, introduced himself, and shook hands with everyone.

Later Billy stood and introduced all the members of the team in glowing terms. Our Canadian friends were informed what "outstanding" individuals we were, for Billy spared no adjectives in his generosity. I meanwhile was asking myself, *Why does he do this? We're not that remarkable. He is the one who is remarkable; we should be introducing him.* But that was Billy's way. He was always taking the spotlight off himself and putting it on someone else. One result—naturally, we all felt great.

Allan Emery, president of the board of directors of the Billy Graham Association, is quoted by biographer Martin as saying, "'Billy has one of those rare qualities that the greatest of leaders have—that of being able to share the glory. He never stints in the praise he gives anyone.'"[8]

Put this down for leadership: A leader cares about his followers and builds them up. He draws attention to them, not to himself. That's Billy.

In another crusade a young man told me he wanted to meet Dr. Graham. He said he was interested in becoming an international evangelist, and he was keen to learn from Dr. Graham how he could do it. I told him I would try to help him—that the members of our team would be at a certain house after that evening's meeting, and perhaps Billy could go there and could spare a moment for the young man.

About 10:30 that night at the private home, the doorbell rang, and our host said someone wished to speak with me. It was the young man. I told him if he would kindly wait just outside, I would see what I could do.

When I told Billy that a young man who wanted to become an evangelist wished to speak to him, Billy immediately got to his feet. He said with a smile, "That's what I'm here for." When we reached the door, no one was there! We walked down the sidewalk toward the street. Finally a car door opened, and the young man condescended to emerge and come halfway up the sidewalk, where the interview took place.

"How can I become an international evangelist like you?" he asked.

"I have no idea," said Billy. "I never in the world expected to become an international evangelist. That's God's doing, not mine."

"How should I go about it?" the young man persisted.

"Just pray. Get a couple of your friends to pray with you. Ask your pastor to pray with you. Put it all in God's hands. It's His decision."

By this time I felt we had been gracious enough and suggested we return inside. When Billy and I reentered the house, he thanked me for what I had done. I wasn't too happy about it. If the young man ever became an international evangelist, I missed it somehow.

Put this down for leadership: A good leader will go out of his way to help people even when they don't deserve it or seem to appreciate it. That's Billy.

While at *Decision*, I published a speech by a prominent Christian citizen. I had not heard the speech, but my associates had. When the text came across my desk, I deleted two controversial paragraphs because the gentleman expressed an opinion that I knew Billy Graham did not share. I was ever conscious that it was Billy's magazine I was editing. A galley of the article was sent to the speaker for his approval. He sent it back insisting that I reinstate the two paragraphs, or else he would withdraw it from publication altogether.

We were now approaching a deadline involving millions of copies of our magazine. It was too late to talk to Billy. Accordingly, I did what I had to do—went to press with the two paragraphs deleted.

When this issue of the magazine appeared, a copy was sent to the author of the article. He did not respond to me; instead he called Billy Graham. In due course I received a telephone call from Billy. He told me the man said I had disobeyed his explicit instructions.

Instead of chiding me, Billy defended me. As I remember, he told me he had said to the gentleman that he had the highest confidence in me as his editor. He had seen me under pressure "hundreds of times," and He had always found me acting with integrity. He apologized and called the whole matter unfortunate, and that was it.

What a relief! I knew those paragraphs had no business appearing in Billy Graham's magazine. But Billy said something else to me before he hung up: "Next time, Woody, don't get caught so close to the deadline. Protect yourself."

Put this down for leadership: A good leader supports those he leads, takes their part, and if possible defends them, even when it's inconvenient to do so. That's Billy.

I have watched people stand on Billy's crusade platform and have heard them say things I knew he didn't agree with—things that made me almost cringe. I have watched other people take advantage of Billy's platform to advertise their own ministries at length and never mention Billy's generosity. In every case Billy overlooked the matter and acted the perfect gentleman.

Put this down for leadership: A good leader overlooks the things that don't matter, even when they annoy him. He saves himself for the big issues. That's Billy.

Once in Minneapolis at a staff meeting I heard him explain how he operates as a team player. He said he knew other evangelists who hired people and then spent time continually checking up on the employees. His own method, he said, was to invite a man to take an assignment, pray with him, hand him his task, and then let him fulfil it. ("Turn him loose," was Billy's expression.) He said he expected to hear good reports of the person's work and its results—and almost invariably he did.

Put this down for leadership: A good leader has absolute confidence in the people working on the team and gives them freedom to work. That's Billy.

When the twentieth century reached the three-quarter mark, Billy Graham and his team spent five days in Rio de Janeiro, Brazil. This evangelistic crusade set attendance records that are still unbroken. On Sunday, October 6, 1975, a total of 230,000 people filled the Maracanà, the world's largest stadium, to hear the Gospel preached. It was among the most bubbly, joyful meetings in the history of evangelism. When the choir sang, the audience joined in. When the soloists sang, the audience applauded each verse. When someone on the platform prayed, they all prayed. Several bands kept playing intermittently throughout the afternoon, often at the same time, whether they were supposed to or not.

Neyde dos Santos, a resident of Rio, and her son were a part of that vast audience. As a young married woman, she had heard Billy fifteen years before in 1960 when he had spoken at a Baptist World Alliance rally in the Maracanà. At that time she had yielded her life to Jesus Christ. Two days later she gave birth to a son. In appreciation for what God had done in her life through His servant, she named her son Billy Graham dos Santos.

Five months before our team arrived in Rio, Billy dos Santos, now fourteen years of age, went forward himself to receive Jesus as his Savior at a service in the First Baptist Church of Niteroi, pastored by Dr. Nilson Fanini, the crusade chairman. By October 1975, when our crusade began, young Billy had already composed several hymns.

I was introduced to Neyde dos Santos and young Billy at the Maracanà Stadium amid the huge crowd. I thought that Billy senior ought to know about his young namesake. Russ Busby, our team photographer, helped me steer the young Billy to the platform, where he was warmly welcomed by the evangelist. We obtained a fine photo of Billy Graham standing with his arm around young Billy Graham dos Santos in front of 230,000 people. (That photograph is now the frontispiece for this book.)

Put this down for leadership: No matter how important his or her duties may be, a leader will always try to find time to do small favors for ordinary people.

To sum up, leadership is a function, not a title or a list of qualities. Author Fred Smith says that one is only a leader if people are following him or her.[9] If no one is following, there is no leader. Billy Graham is a leader of millions, but like his Master, he seeks to make himself last, not first.

Dear, Mr. Grham,

Sir, we have never
met but you have done a
lot for our family, Mom and
Dad nevery went to church
untill they heard you on
TV and now they go every
Sunday and Wednesday. They
try to live right evething is
so much better.

In Christain
Love,
Kitty Wilcox

Twenty-Two

GREATNESS

~

YOURS, O LORD, IS THE GREATNESS,
THE POWER AND THE GLORY.

—1 CHRONICLES 29:11

Many times I have puzzled over this question: When one is close to greatness, does any of it ever rub off? Is there fallout? Does the nearness to greatness make one, if not great, at least a near-great?

As I have indicated, Billy and I have had a cordial, if infrequent, relationship over many years. When he sees me, he often greets me with, "How are you, beloved?" I like being around someone like that. I don't recall anyone else using exactly those words with me, and I have certainly been addressed in ways a lot less favorable. But much as I would like to think that greatness is communicable if you get close, I have to acknowledge each morning as I look into the mirror that the prospect is dicey. The likelihood of greatness is like the danger from a satellite out of orbit—it may come down and hit you but probably won't.

Shakespeare once wrote that "some men are born great, some achieve greatness, and some have greatness thrust upon them."[1] He should have added, "And a lot of men—and women—ain't, and don't."

But hold on. The Bible does not classify greatness the way Shakespeare does. There is another source of greatness that may explain Billy Graham and may even hold out hope for you and me. That other source is "the love of God poured out into our hearts by the Holy Spirit which is given to us."[2] Alongside this spiritual source, all other "credentials" based on birth, gender, achievement, chance, fate, and luck fade into insignificance for those who know the love of God in Christ Jesus.

Marcus Tullius Cicero, sometimes called the greatest of the ancient Romans, once wrote, "No man was ever great without divine inspiration."[3] Good man, Tully! (That's how the scholars refer to him). Tully's criterion, given so long ago, would toss out many of the "Persons of the Year" that *Time* magazine insists on choosing each January. He would say they are not great at all. But my guess is that Tully would make an exception of the issue that carried Billy Graham's picture as "Man of the Year!"

Another interesting quote about greatness is attributed to a noble French lady, Madame Cornuel: "No man is a hero to his valet."[4] Often true, no doubt, but surely one of the reasons a person is great is precisely because he (or she) *is* a hero to his valet (or her *femme-de-chambre*).

Billy Graham has no valet, but he has a lot of employees. I have known personally most of the men and women who served on Billy's traveling team during and since the years when I edited his magazine, including those closest to him. I am convinced that all of them were and are thoroughly devoted to Billy, even those who have left the team. (Billy often brings them back.) Billy on his part has always been extravagant in his praises of those who have worked for him. Does that sound unusual? Remember, we are discussing greatness. Truly great people really are different. If the New Testament tells us anything, it tells us that Jesus did communicate greatness to at least some of His disciples.

Lest you think I am trying to include myself in this discussion, I shall interrupt with a story. Once during a Billy Graham crusade in Denver, Colorado, I needed an overhead crowd photo for *Decision*, and I was told that none had been scheduled. I thought that a pity, as Billy was preaching in Denver's picturesque Mile-High Stadium. Accordingly, on Sunday afternoon I engaged a small plane and a photographer (Russ Busby was busy) and ordered them to fly over the stadium for some shots.

The Sunday afternoon service began, and just as the crusade choir and George Beverly Shea, soloist, rose to sing, my single-engine wonder came buzzing over the stadium at 800 feet. The pilot made one pass, and then to my excruciating embarrassment, he flew back back and forth over the stadium several times, completely drowning out the music. Cliff Barrows, our beloved song leader, had to apologize to the crowd and then state that at Mr. Graham's request, the anthem would be repeated, which it was.

Oh, how I wished to be somewhere else! Greatness? I felt about as great as a flea on a camel's back. Sooner or later I knew that the culprit would be flushed out—me. One of my fellow team members described it this way: "Woody told the pilot to make one pass and get six pictures. Instead he made six passes and got one picture." But, strangely, no rebukes from anyone ever came my way. Billy did not mention the subject.

Another characteristic of greatness is the ability to get along with other people. For example, General Dwight D. Eisenhower was a splendid leader of the free world even before he became president of the United States. He managed to mold together as leaders of the Allied forces warriors as disparate as Generals George Patton and Sir Bernard Montgomery. As Allies they made a magnificent team, and under Eisenhower, together with the Russians, they defeated the Nazi armies and smashed Hitler.

Billy Graham has Ike's wonderful ability to mix with people and make friends, whatever their background. I am not just quoting others, for I have known both men.

I also had on May 7, 1963, in Cambridge, England, what was perhaps the last interview with Professor C. S. Lewis before his death. Lewis, whose Christian writings have attracted readers worldwide, was an Anglican layman. In the Church of England today many express disapproval of Billy Graham and his ministry. Such persons would consider him anything but great. Let me therefore quote an excerpt from that interview with Lewis just as it was published in

1970 in the book, *God in the Dock, Essays in Theology and Ethics,*
by C. S. Lewis:

> Wirt: Do you approve of men such as Bryan Green and Billy
> Graham asking people to come to a point of decision regard-
> ing the Christian life?
>
> Lewis [after affirming his approval]: I had the pleasure of
> meeting Billy Graham once. We had dinner together during
> his visit to Cambridge University in 1955, while he was con-
> ducting a mission to students. I thought he was a very mod-
> est and a very sensible man, and I liked him very much
> indeed.[5]

Greatness often does reciprocate greatness. I will give you some
other brief examples:

Pearl Goode, the elderly woman of prayer who followed Billy
from crusade to crusade from 1954 until her passing in 1972, living
in small hotels and praying for Billy in seclusion. In Copenhagen she
did her praying in a tub of hot water to keep warm.

Cardinal Wojtyla of Poland, who warmly supported Billy's
preaching mission to Krakow in 1978. Just before Billy arrived, the
cardinal went to Rome where he was elected Pope John Paul II.

Muhammad Ali, the prize fighter, who paid a visit to Billy and
Ruth at their North Carolina home and was astonished when Billy
met him personally at the Asheville airport and drove him in his own
car to Montreat.

Here is a quite different example: In a South American city a
young rabbi came to the platform at the close of an evangelistic service and confronted Billy.

"I suppose," he said (I am not quoting him exactly), "according
to your theology, you would consign me to hell because I am a Jew
and you are a Christian."

Billy replied (and I am quoting exactly), "Sir, I am delighted to
meet you. We worship the same God. There is just this difference
between us: You believe that the Messiah is yet to come. I believe
He has already come."

In many ways Billy fits the classic description of a gentleman from the hand of John Henry Newman, a distinguished nineteenth-century English churchman:

> The true gentleman carefully avoids all clashing of opinion, or suspicion, or gloom, or resentment; his concern being to make everyone at ease. He is tender toward the bashful, gentle toward the distant, and merciful toward the absurd. He guards against unseasonable allusions, or topics which may irritate. He makes light of favors while he does them, and seems to be receiving when he is conferring. He never speaks of himself except when compelled, never defends himself by a mere retort. He is never mean or little in his disputes, never takes unfair advantage or insinuates evil. He observes the maxim of the ancient sage, that we should ever conduct ourselves toward our enemy as if he were one day to be our friend. He has too much good sense to be affronted by insults, is scrupulous about not imputing motives to those who interfere with him, and interprets everything for the best.[6]

I am quite aware that when Billy Graham has finished his course, there will be a great outpouring around the world of eulogies, encomiums, and panegyrics in praise of his life. The lengthy obituaries are already in print and on file. Impressive testimonials to his achievements will then be spoken in halls and palaces. Documents will be published and medals struck. One reason for these pages is that I think Billy and Ruth deserve to hear some of that adulation while they are still alive, even though they might modestly object.

Another reason for writing is that when I first began my association with Billy, I was not convinced of his greatness because of something that took place in 1959. After our return from Tasmania, Billy asked me to remain in Melbourne and spend some time in bookstores and libraries gathering material for a book he was planning to write. (The book eventually appeared in 1965 under the title *World Aflame*.) In the following two weeks I accumulated what I thought was some valuable information about the political standoff between Eastern and Western Europe. The Soviets not only had the nuclear bomb, but they were said to have a hundred thousand spies in New York City alone. Castro was installing missile launchers. China was threatening Taiwan. Tito was defying Stalin. The outbreak of war seemed very real.

I also gathered important data about the current social and moral crises facing what we still called the "Allied nations." After preparing this material in typewritten form, I took it in my briefcase on the flight from Sydney to Auckland. During that journey Billy came and sat beside me with a smile and asked how I had made out in Melbourne. We spent perhaps ten minutes going through my typewritten pages together. He expressed deep interest. Then he stood up, smiled, and said, "Sherwood, you've done an excellent job. Now you're going to have to sit down and explain all this to me."

He returned to his seat, leaving me stunned. What did he mean? Was he implying that he was unaware of what was going on in the world of 1959? Or that I somehow possessed superior insight? *Well, I thought with a touch of ego, I suppose it's conceivable. But is he really that naive?*

Looking back, I have had a few chuckles, not at Billy's naiveté, but at my own. I was soon to learn that Billy Graham knew far more than I did about what was going on. He talked and still talks regularly with kings and queens, presidents and cardinals and statesmen, economists and atomic scientists. He is consulted by social experts, both men and women. He visits the Pentagon and the Congress and the World Council of Churches. He fine-tunes the media as no one else does. He reads important books and listens to his brilliant wife.

Yes, Billy is great. I was misled by his humble and ingenuous approach, but I know better now.

But what manner of greatness is it that Billy has? In the jacket copy of one book about him, the publisher writes that the author "describes how Graham's lifelong ambition 'to do something great for God' led him to organize mammoth international conferences that have helped forge a coalition crucial to the worldwide spread of Evangelical Christianity, and to pursue efforts to enhance religious freedom in the Soviet bloc nations and the People's Republic of China. . . ." The publisher adds, "From this book readers will gain a better understanding of the most successful evangelist in Christian history."

But is that all there was to it—mere ambition? Is that what motivated Billy? He had become a follower of Jesus. Is that what motivated Jesus? Let's set the record straight. Factually and theologically, all Billy Graham did was to get out of God's way. He laid his life at the altar and made himself an empty vessel for the Holy Spirit to fill and use. If you don't believe that, ask Billy. His lifelong ambition was and is to let God run his life. No one can possibly understand the "most successful evangelist in Christian history" unless one knows that Billy considers such titles good for selling books and little else.

God is love.[7] It was God's loving desire to make His servant an instrument to win millions of people to Himself. That's why He poured out His love into Billy's heart. Billy Graham saw what the Holy Spirit was doing and wanted done, and he showed up for work. A Scottish editor, J. W. Stevenson, expressed it this way:

> Every night . . . he made hundreds of people feel that he was speaking straight to their hearts. The Spirit of God was speaking through him, using him, by-passing him, turning even his mistakes to account, all the time reminding him that this was not his doing, but God's. This is, perhaps, his greatest power. To be with him even for a short time is to get a sense of a man wholly committed, a single-minded man; it shames and shakes one as no amount of ability and cleverness can do. Here is someone who has the purity of heart which sees God.[8]

Billy's life, and every believer's life, starts in the throne room of heaven. If there is greatness, the greatness is God's.

C. S. Lewis once wrote, "The salvation of a single soul is more important than the production or preservation of all the epics and tragedies in the world."[9] Such is the arithmetic of joy, and joy, as Lewis said, is the serious business of heaven (Luke 15:7).[10] This book is not a tribute to a man; it is written to glorify God and magnify His greatness in deigning to use the elder son of Frank and Morrow Graham to fulfil His own desires for our generation.

One way to measure greatness is by a person's family. It is not infallible—Jesus' own family did not seem to understand Him during His years of ministry. Some Christians have made a great spiritual impact on their generation, only to find their own children a keen disappointment to them. I have also known Christian couples who never achieved much in this life, but whose children grew up to be marvelous men and women of God.

Ruth Graham, and Billy when he was not traveling, brought up five children, all of whom are lovers of Jesus Christ and recognized as outstanding leaders on several continents. To write about these sons and daughters (all of whom are my friends) is not within the domain of this book. But because I know and admire them all, I at least want to mention them. God has blessed them all with strong faith and marvelous gifts.

Virginia ("Gigi") Tchivijian has become a superb, distinctive author and speaker and has a wide following of her own. She also has a bountiful family and a talented, professional husband.

Anne Lotz too has a noble family and husband and has in recent years developed an astonishing international gospel ministry of her own. She speaks to large, eager throngs wherever she goes.

Ruth ("Bunny") McIntyre and I became friends at the Billy Graham Pavilion at the New York World's Fair of 1964. With a beautiful family, she has become a fine writer and skillful editor for national publishing houses.

Franklin (William Franklin III) has developed into a son worthy of his illustrious parents, and his own thrilling story has won national applause. Read *Rebel with a Cause*. That's all I can say at this time.

Ned, the youngest (Nelson Edman), and I have known each other a long time. He and I flew the Atlantic together when he was three. As president of "East Gates" ministries, which distributes Bibles, Ned is God's man of the hour both in China and North Korea.

"Behold, children are a heritage of the Lord," says the psalmist. They are also a clue to greatness.

Twenty-Three

THE ROYAL MUSKETEERS

~

Give me ten men who are stout-hearted men,
who will march for the Christ they adore;
Start me with ten who are Spirit-filled men,
and I'll soon give you ten thousand more.
—S. E. W., WITH APOLOGIES TO THE COMPOSER

ALL THESE WERE . . . CHOICE MEN,
MIGHTY MEN OF VALOR, CHIEF LEADERS.

—1 CHRONICLES 7:40

The human race has always loved teams of "a few good men."
We adore them and make heroes of them. Jesus and eleven of
His first disciples have captured and held the imagination of billions
of believers over the last two millennia. Lowly at the beginning, they
rose to the heights, and today they are the supreme team of all time.
All are still remembered with gratitude by Christians around the
world. We revere them as apostles of Jesus Christ and heralds of His
Gospel of salvation.

Centuries before Jesus walked the earth, His ancestor King David
had his own mighty men, warriors whose accomplishments are
immortalized in the pages of the Old Testament. In particular three
men of war—Josheb-Basshebeth the Tachmonite, Eleazar son of
Dodo, and Shammah son of Agee—are remembered because they
performed incredible feats of valor in David's battles against the
Philistines.[1]

In the annals of Roman history three romantic names stand out.
They are the valiant soldier-heroes—Horatius, Spurius Lartius, and
Herminius—who (according to historian Macauley) saved the city

against an invading army by guarding the bridge across the Tiber River until it could be cut down on the Roman side.

Greek history has its seven magnificent heroes—Adrastus, Amphiaraus, and their fellow warriors—who led a failed expedition to dethrone Eteocles, the ruler of Thebes. Aeschylus wrote a heroic drama about the *Seven Against Thebes*.

Early English history has taken us to Camelot, a city long lost in the mists of time, where King Arthur and his knights gathered at the famous Round Table, then rode out and wrought amazing deeds of goodness and mercy. Who can forget those knights—Sir Gawain, Sir Percivale, Sir Galahad, and Sir Gareth? In Britain people still name their children after them.

In 1885 the great English cricketer C. T. Studd, his friend Stanley P. Smith, stroke of the Cambridge Boat, and five other young Christian men created a sensation by offering themselves as missionaries to China. One was the stroke of a "trial eight," one was a Dragoon guardsman, and another an officer of the Royal Volunteers. The eventual sailing of "the Cambridge Seven" for China caused a student revival to break out in the colleges and universities of the British Isles.[2]

Andrew Carnegie, the multimillionaire humanitarian and manufacturer who headed the United States Steel Corporation, once predicted that if everything he owned were taken away from him and destroyed, in ten years he would have it all back. His one stipulation: "Just leave me my men."

For over fifty years Billy Graham has conducted his international ministry for Jesus Christ in association with a team of men. Principal Gilbert Kirby of London Bible College called it "the most effective small team I have ever seen. You can liken it to the apostolic party with Paul, traveling around Asia Minor, going to strategic places. I don't know when there has been another small team like it. Certainly not in this century."[3]

Some of the men on the original Billy Graham team, which began to be formed in the mid-1940s, have been together for half a century and are still evangelizing to the glory of God. Rather than attempt to profile them properly, I will just speak of them briefly as my friends.

Royal Musketeers: The Graham team in 1966—
(l. to r.) Grady Wilson, T.W. Wilson, Cliff Barrows, Billy
Graham, George Beverly Shea, Leighton Ford. Seated: Tedd Smith.

Because the whole team embraces so many men and women, I will limit my remarks to particular teammates who were active when I joined them in 1959 and with whom I worked for the next seventeen years. Most of them are alive at this writing, and several are still active on the team.

The four best-known members are Cliff Barrows, George Beverly Shea, Tedd Smith, and Grady Wilson. Since 1950 this immensely popular platform band has toured the world with Billy—Cliff being the impresario and music leader, Bev the soloist, and Tedd the pianist and accompanist. Grady filled a special role as Billy's tour manager, traveling aide, bodyguard, and (on occasion) court jester. He was promoted to glory in 1987. The other three continue in active roles at this writing.

Three other names, not so universally known, belong with the original team. George Wilson was the BGEA treasurer almost from the very start. Walter Smyth, who joined in 1950, became in time the director of crusades. T. W. Wilson, who had helped Billy earlier as a school vice president in Minnesota and subsequently during the 1949-50 crusades, came back from an Alabama pastorate in 1964 to be Billy's close personal assistant. These men formed the nucleus of the ministry that led well over a million people into a saving relationship with Jesus Christ.

The bonds of love in Christ held these seven men together, with others, through half a century of a most strenuous global evangelistic effort. Those bonds are still strong and deep. They include not only the men but also their wives, children, grandchildren, and in some cases great-grandchildren. Altogether these seven, the inner core of the Billy Graham team, are a fascinating and dedicated band of Christian men. I never get over the thrill of having known and worked with them.

To use an analogy, when my present pastor, Mike MacIntosh, was young and unconverted, he yearned to become the "fifth Beatle." He listened to the Beatles' music, watched their movies by the hour, daydreamed, and even tried to work his way across the Atlantic to join them in England. Today, needless to say, he is a different person. He never became a Beatle, but he pastors the largest church in San Diego, California, has preached around the world, and is one of the great church builders and philanthropists of our time. (And he has also become a good musician!)

By contrast, I too had daydreams as a young man, but never could I have imagined that God would make me part of the Billy Graham team. Until certain godly people took hold of me, I had all the spirituality of a centipede. Even now, in my mid-eighties and retired, those years with Billy still seem to me incredible. I take my joy from the fact that all of the team are my warm friends and buddies. They took me as I am and treated me as a brother in Christ. In return, I vowed to God that when I became editor of *Decision*, I would give them hearty and plentiful support in the pages of the magazine—which I did.

Here are further descriptions of Billy Graham's team, men of strong hearts whose love for Jesus made them one:

Cliff Barrows. The son of Christian parents, a rugged Californian

still strong and handsome in his seventies, Cliff is the program director and master of ceremonies at the Billy Graham crusades. He has
led millions of singers all over the world in rendering choral praises
to God. He has also produced the *Hour of Decision* radio broadcast,
participates on several boards and ministries of the Billy Graham
Association, edits songbooks, and is himself a fine evangelist,
preacher, and musician. In 1988 he was inducted into the Nashville
Gospel Music Association Hall of Fame. But what people love most
about Cliff is his cheerful, friendly, helpful spirit toward everyone. He
sets the tone of the crusades. Cliff and I share this experience, that
both our wives succumbed to cancer, and we are now each happily
remarried. For me Cliff's friendship has ripened with the years. What
a winsome guy! Billy Graham told 10,000 evangelists gathered in
Amsterdam in 1986, "God has given me mighty men, but the might-
iest of all has been Cliff Barrows."

George Beverly Shea. "Bev," a Canadian by birth, comes from a
godly minister's home. He is a big man with a big heart, another wid-
ower who has happily remarried. Right from the start in Australia in
1959, I found Bev the most amiable and endearing of colleagues. His
bass-baritone voice, recorded in hundreds of songs, has lifted the
hearts of millions to God. He is known, and has been known for
decades, as "America's beloved gospel singer." Bev won a Grammy
Award in 1965, was elected to the Nashville Gospel Music Hall of
Fame in 1987, and has been recording on RCA, Word, and Star Song
labels. He has been heard in concerts around the world. Even more
than his talent, those who are close to him love him for his warm piety
and humble mien. Now in his late eighties, Bev still sings a song of
God's love at crusades just before Billy begins to preach his sermon.

Tedd Smith. Tedd Smith, also a Canadian-born Christian, won his
first gold medal in piano at the age of nine at Canada's Peel Music
Festival. Later he graduated from the Royal Conservatory of Music
in Toronto. Tedd is a gifted musician and composer and an interna-
tionally known concert artist. Ruth and I have visited him and his
lovely wife, Thelma, in their home, and he has written songs and covered stories for me as an editor. After forty-five years as Billy Graham's
pianist, he has recently changed positions and is now producing the

programs of Billy's crusade ministry. Tedd's *Tobago Suite*, composed after the team paid an evangelistic visit to the Caribbean in 1959, contains some of my favorite music. His exquisite artistry and his devotion to Christ have brought a quality dimension to the team.

T. W. (Thomas Walter) Wilson. "T," as his friends call him affectionately, is first of all one of America's renowned preachers. He is also Billy Graham's personal assistant, his equerry, his bodyguard, his right-hand man, his associate evangelist, his present traveling companion, and generally is perhaps the most indispensable person on the team after the evangelist. He holds many positions of responsibility, including the oversight of Billy's radio stations. The son of a Charlotte, North Carolina, plumber who was a friend of Billy's father, "T" formerly pastored Baptist churches in Georgia and Alabama. He was vice president of Youth for Christ International and vice president of Northwestern Schools. He cares for his present duties on the team with Christian love, sound judgment, and a genial disposition that make all of us on the team love him.

Grady B. Wilson. Grady, "T's" younger brother, left us for heaven in the early fall of 1987. Grady, as a boy, went forward with Billy Graham in November 1934 at that famous revival service in Charlotte, North Carolina, when Mordecai Ham was the evangelist. Billy and Grady remained the closest of friends and traveled the world together until Grady's final illness and homegoing. It is hard to do justice to Grady Wilson in a few words. Time after time he helped me when I was in awkward situations. As an associate evangelist, he was splendid; as a salty humorist, he was beyond compare. Grady kept not only Billy, but everyone else, in good humor. Yet he had a mind like a rapier, knew exactly what to tell the media, and had an unerring instinct to protect Billy Graham. Paul Harvey, the commentator, once said that Grady had more horse sense than all the rest of the team put together.

Walter Herbert Smyth. Walter is known as Billy Graham's crusades architect all over the world. Quiet, tactful, effective, a minister and former vice president of Youth for Christ International, Walter joined the team as director of film distribution in 1950 at Billy's request. Before long he succeeded Jerry Beavan as director of crusades and then became Billy Graham's vice president for international relations. A superb negotiator who traveled the globe tirelessly, Walter laid the foundation for Billy's great world congresses on evangelism in Berlin, Lausanne, and Amsterdam, and still later for his ministry behind the Iron Curtain in Romania, Hungary, and the former Soviet Union. When he directed the 1958 San Francisco crusade, Walter not only preached in my church in east Oakland, but he also opened publishing doors for my book *Crusade at the Golden Gate*. The book in turn led to my joining the team. Ruth and I pray daily for our friend Walter as he recovers slowly from his recent strokes.

George McConnell Wilson. When I first arrived in Minneapolis, Minnesota, in February 1959, George Wilson was an administrative giant and just about the most important person in the Twin Cities. As head of the Billy Graham Evangelistic Association's main office, secretary and treasurer of the board of directors, and corporate vice president, George talked daily with Billy Graham. He handled the finances, conducted an astonishingly successful direct-mail operation, and ran a tight ship. He was my boss. A rugged Baptist layman (though he is licensed to preach), he viewed me at first with some skepticism, but gave me the freedom to prove myself as the editor of Billy's magazine. George and his wife, Helen, were generous, kind, and gracious to me, to my late wife, Winola, and to our son Alexander. He supported good works around the world, and today he continues to be active in the Lord's work despite his confinement to a wheelchair as he recovers from a stroke.

Akbar Abdul-Haqq. When Billy Graham made his four-week tour of India in 1956, his interpreter was Dr. Haqq, who held a Ph.D. from Northwestern University in Chicago. A Methodist minister, Akbar became president of the Henry Martyn School of Islamics in Aligarh, Northern India. Billy invited Akbar to join his team as an associate evangelist and bring his large family to America. In the thirty years that have passed, Akbar has faithfully ministered the Gospel in his unique and effective way to millions of people in India, while also preaching Jesus Christ all over the Western world. The family home is in Burnsville, Minnesota.

Donald L. Bailey. Don began his team relationship in 1954 as one of Billy's traveling film exhibitors. Born of Christian parents in Pennsylvania, educated in New York and South Carolina, he met his wife, Robbie, in New Orleans while serving in uniform. After the Korean War, Don went from film exhibiting to helping build the Billy Graham North Carolina radio stations, WFGW/WMIT. Subsequently he became Billy's gifted radio and public relations executive and manager of the team office in Atlanta. Leaving for a three-year stint in hospital public relations in Nashville, Don was summoned back in 1989 to become program director at the new Billy Graham Training Center at The Cove, Asheville, North Carolina.

David M. Barr. A Baptist preacher, Barr has given the best years of his life to the spreading of the Gospel of Jesus Christ through Billy Graham films produced by World Wide Pictures. WWP, the cinematic arm of the BGEA, has brought hundreds of thousands of viewers to commit their lives to Christ. Starting in 1952 as a distributor-on-wheels, Dave became director in charge of twenty-eight full-time exhibitors in fifty states and Canada. He was then assigned to the whole world! For years Dave traveled on six continents, using subtitles for viewers in Swahili, Samoan, Hindi, etc., exhibiting films, and counseling inquirers. He still preaches a lot and lives with his family in Pennsylvania.

Ralph Bell. A scion of American slaves who escaped across the border to Canada 150 years ago, Ralph was a prison chaplain in Los Angeles when Billy Graham invited him to join the team as an associate evangelist. Ralph holds a degree from Fuller Theological Seminary and has conducted evangelistic crusades around the world, bringing Christ to thousands of people of every race and color. A man with a keen mind and a loving heart, he had a specially anointed ministry to Australian aborigines and to students in Papua New Guinea. In 1995, when Billy Graham collapsed briefly during a speech in Toronto, Canada, it was Ralph who stood in the gap and for three nights proclaimed the gospel message to his fellow Canadians. Hundreds of them walked forward at his invitation and committed their lives to Christ.

William F. (Bill) Brown. A native of Pennsylvania, a Bible college

graduate, Bill Brown was hired by Walter Smyth in 1952 to distrib-
ute and show Graham films in churches. While Bill was conducting
a week's premier showing of the film *Souls in Conflict* at Carnegie
Hall in New York City in 1954, Billy Graham brought over the beautiful star of the film, British actress Joan Winmill, a Harringay crusade convert. Bill and Joan fell in love and were married in April
1955. After their marriage Bill directed citywide crusades, including
London '66 and '67 and New York '69. In 1970 he became president of World Wide Pictures, producing some great films such as *The
Hiding Place* and *Joni*. Bill still works with Billy Graham, and Joan
has authored nineteen inspirational books.

Russell Busby. Some forty years ago, during the Oklahoma City
crusade of 1956, Russ Busby came to the attention of George Wilson,
Billy Graham's treasurer, who was looking for a photographer who
loved the Lord. Soon Russ, his wife, Doris, and four children moved
to Minnesota, and he began his remarkable and indispensable career
as a photographer with the Billy Graham Association. He accompanied Billy on most of his trips. Several million excellent photographs
later, he is still girdling the globe, recording history by camera, and
making his own unique observations on the Christian life. Russ and
I are fast friends. We worked on this book the way we worked as an
editorial team for many years. He and his wife live in southern
California.

John R. Corts, Jr. John is president and chief operating officer of
the Billy Graham Evangelistic Association, a position he has held
since 1983. Born in Indiana, he was educated at the same Trinity
College that Billy attended. After being ordained and pastoring
churches in Florida, he became in 1962 executive director of Tampa
Youth for Christ. Two years later he joined the Billy Graham team
but then returned to pastoring in 1980. John was chosen to become
president of Trinity, which honored him with a doctorate. He filled
key roles in Billy Graham's international conferences in Amsterdam,
after which he was appointed head of the BGEA. His family home is
now in Minneapolis.

John W. Dillon. For many years John Dillon, a Wesleyan
preacher from South Dakota, held one of the more important port-

folios in Billy Graham's program—training ministers in the work of evangelism. Under John's direction, Schools of Evangelism were conducted all over North America as well as in Britain and Ireland, with huge throngs of pastors attending. In the fall of 1961 John was pastoring a church in Aberdeen, South Dakota, when Leighton Ford held a crusade there. Shortly afterward John joined the team as a film exhibitor for World Wide Pictures, covering the upper Midwest. He later became director of the team associate evangelists' program and in 1980 took over the important leadership of the Schools of Evangelism. Illness took his wife, Louise, in 1988. Now happily remarried and retired, John and his wife, Betty, make their home in North Carolina.

Robert Oscar Ferm. Dr. Robert Ferm was the biblical scholar on the Billy Graham team. Quiet, congenial, erudite, beloved, he helped establish Billy's reputation as a genuine theologian and biblical apologist in the historic mainline of Paul, Augustine, Luther, Spurgeon, Kuyper, and Machen—as well as an evangelist in the tradition of Paul, Chrysostom, Wesley, Whitefield, Finney, and Moody. Dr. Ferm did it with well-researched, strong books, *Cooperative Evangelism, The Psychology of Christian Conversion,* and *Do the Billy Graham Converts Last?* A Baptist pastor for several years, executive vice president of John Brown University, dean of Northwestern Schools, and dean of students at Houghton College, he led pastors' conferences for Billy, helped to found his Schools of Evangelism, and was one of *Decision*'s first editors.

Leighton F. S. Ford. A strikingly impressive man, Leighton is married to Billy Graham's sister Jean. For thirty years he was vice president of the Billy Graham Evangelistic Association and an associate evangelist on the team. Leighton's clear-cut gospel message has been received with tremendous enthusiasm all over the world, most notably in his native Canada, the United States, Australia, and New Zealand. A loving husband and devoted father, author, and popular speaker, Dr. Ford is genial, compassionate, and highly perceptive. He left the Billy Graham team (with Billy's blessing) in 1986 to launch Leighton Ford Ministries. This successful independent Christian work, in Leighton's words, "focuses on helping young evangelism leaders to lead more *like* Jesus and to lead more *to* Jesus."

Roy Gustafson. In 1965 Associate Evangelist Roy Gustafson took Winola and me on one of the hundreds of Holy Land tours he has conducted since joining the Billy Graham team in 1959. I learned what a superb gift of Bible teaching God has given him. Author, musician, preacher, husband, and father, he has taught the Bible in his inimitable style to tens of thousands of people around the world. Roy and Billy were fellow students at Florida Bible Institute. Years later it was Roy's Spirit-led discipling that God used to bring Billy's elder son Franklin into His kingdom. Roy continues active in his teaching ministry, and at the time of this writing is fulfilling an assignment in a Bible College in Malawi (formerly Nyasaland), Africa.

Henry Holley. Henry made his first contact with Billy Graham in 1958 and became an active volunteer at crusades while still on duty with the United States Marine Corps. Upon retirement from the military in 1967 with the rank of master sergeant, he began serving full time as crusade director in many parts of the world. For nearly three decades Henry has been a key field director for Billy in some of his greatest overseas ministries, notably in England, France, Australia, Jamaica, Philippines, Finland, Japan, Korea, Hong Kong, Taiwan, and Brazil. A brilliant strategist and beloved husband and father, Henry continues his active ministry as international crusade director and special assistant to Billy Graham.

Sterling W. Huston. A graduate of the University of Maine, Sterling became an industrial engineer at Eastman Kodak before directing Youth for Christ in Rochester, New York. He joined the Billy Graham team in 1966. One of his first assignments was to visit church leaders in Nassau, Bahamas, in preparation for a John Wesley White crusade. Winola and I accompanied Sterling and Esther, his bride of eighteen months, visiting the Anglican bishop and other spiritual leaders. One of Dr. White's greatest crusades came as a result in 1967. As teacher, negotiator, director of Billy Graham's North American crusades, and author of two excellent books on crusade evangelism, Dr. Sterling Huston has made an impressive contribution to the ministry of the Gospel in our time.

John Innes. England lost a good textile wool sorter in 1958 when twenty-year-old John Innes arrived at Moody Bible Institute, Chicago, for music training. His teacher was Dr. Don Hustad, who at the time was also Billy Graham's crusade organist. After further musical studies, John began playing the piano at Leighton Ford crusade meetings in 1962. When Hustad left for a teaching career, John replaced him at the electric organ. Since Tedd Smith's change of assignments after forty-four years, John is now Billy Graham's team pianist, filling the great meetings with magnificent keyboard music. He says, "I am so grateful to God for putting a song in my heart."

Howard Owen Jones. While playing a saxophone in a jazz orchestra in Oberlin, Ohio, many years ago, Howard courted an attractive girl named Wanda Young. Her Christian witness convinced him to quit the band and accept the Savior. After graduating from Nyack College, they were married, and Howard pastored two Alliance churches. In 1957 Billy Graham invited Howard to become the first Black American associate evangelist on his team. For forty years Howard has led crusades in many parts of the world, including Africa. He is an author, a radio broadcaster, and the first of his race to be inducted into the National Religious Broadcasters' Hall of Fame. A godly wife, five beautiful children, and six grandchildren make him a man richly blessed.

John O. Lenning. A radio engineer who has traveled just about everywhere and done just about everything, John Lenning began life with a strong Christian (Scandinavian) background and spent five years in ministry with the Navigators. He served two years in the military during the Korean War before joining the Graham team as assistant to Cliff Barrows in 1959. For thirty-seven years John has taught training classes, led workshops, directed crusades for associate evangelists, and served as Billy Graham's technical stage manager. His key function is to produce *The Hour of Decision,* Billy's weekly radio program. He holds a degree from Furman University, but his greatest prize is his wife, Jerry, and their four children, all married and all Christians.

Victor B. Nelson. At the time of this writing Dr. Nelson, ninety-three years of age, continues to work at out-of-sight team tasks that have occupied him since 1950. In that year he chaired a Billy Graham crusade in Minneapolis, where he was pastoring a church. In 1961 Victor chaired a second Minneapolis crusade and began occupying a full-time desk in Billy Graham's international headquarters, working on crusade preparation and related tasks. He has helped many people, including myself. His duties took him to Newfoundland, Denmark, West Germany, Singapore, The Netherlands, Switzerland, and other parts of the globe. He was associate director of international congresses in Berlin, Singapore, Amsterdam, and Lausanne. As executive assistant, he still counsels people from his Minneapolis home.

Charles Riggs. Charlie is one of God's most useful servants and one of the most popular men ever to join the Graham team. Discipled through the Navigators while rough-necking in the Pennsylvania oilfields, he has been a team member almost from the beginning. Charlie radiates confidence in the Lord. A man of the Bible and of prayer, he has memorized hundreds of Bible verses and has had us all carrying verse packets in our wallets. He directed many major crusades beginning with the sixteen-week 1957 crusade in New York City, and after forty years, he is still training counselors. He and his wife, LaRue, live in Colorado.

Norman Sanders, Jr. Born in Marion, Alabama, Norman studied at Washington University in St. Louis and Calvary Bible College in Kansas City before he joined Kansas City's Youth for Christ staff. In 1970 he married Cheryl, eldest daughter of Associate Evangelist Howard Jones, and began his BGEA career in Chicago. For twenty-six years Norman traveled to fifty-two cities on four continents, teaching Christian Life and Witness classes and recruiting and training crusade volunteers. At the time of writing, he is director of public relations at The Billy Graham Training Center at The Cove. Norman and Cheryl have two sons, Tim and Ryan.

Larry K. Turner. For most of thirty years Larry Turner was "our man" to Billy Graham—"our man" in Oslo, Gothenburg, Iceland, Essen, Halifax, San Juan, and dozens of other places at home and abroad where Billy's gospel messages were going out. An enormously useful servant of the Lord and a delightful person to know,

Larry grew up in Portland, Oregon, and studied at Portland State, Chicago's North Park Seminary, and Portland's Western Baptist Seminary. Eventually Larry began directing major Billy Graham crusades himself and is currently assistant director of all North American crusades. He and his wife, Nancy, have three children and now live in Fairview, North Carolina.

John Wesley White. John joined the Billy Graham team as an associate evangelist in 1964. A Canadian, holder of a D. Phil. from Oxford, and a most effective preacher, he has won tens of thousands to Christ through his crusades around the world and through his books and his Canadian television ministry. I know of no one with a deeper love for his Lord. Husband of Kathleen, father of four boys, for thirty-two years John has been an author and scholar as well as an indefatigable soul-winner, until a severe stroke felled him during a crusade in 1996. He is now making a courageous and remarkable recovery at his home in Willowdale, Ontario, Canada.

Lee Fisher. Born into a Christian family in Kokomo, Indiana, Lee was graduated from Fort Wayne Bible College. Illness cut short a promising career as itinerant evangelist, and through fellow gospel musician Homer Rodeheaver, he was introduced to Billy Graham and offered a post as research assistant. After moving to North Carolina, Lee became one of Billy's close associates, traveling with him on five continents. After retiring in 1976, Lee, now age 88 and legally blind, lives with his wife, Betty, in Sebastian, Florida. He is the author of several Christian books and many songs.

Charles G. Ward. After years with TEAM in South America, Chuck Ward became Billy's crusade coordinator on his two 1962 Latin American tours. Chuck's next task: dubbing Billy's TV messages into nine languages for viewing in fifty-two countries. Later he headed the massive TV-telephone counseling outreach that brought tens of thousands to Christ. At present Chuck and his wife, Margaret, live in Florida, and he still zealously trains Spanish-speaking volunteers for Billy's crusades. His carefully crafted crusade workers' handbook has become a bestseller.

Twenty-Four

ON THE
LIGHTER SIDE

~

IT WAS RIGHT THAT WE SHOULD MAKE MERRY AND BE GLAD,
FOR YOUR BROTHER WAS DEAD AND IS ALIVE AGAIN,
AND WAS LOST AND IS FOUND.

—LUKE 15:32

Millions of people have heard Billy Graham preach from the pulpit or have listened on radio or watched him on television, but many have never heard him laugh. I can testify that he loves to laugh! At team meetings and with his family, his laughter often rings out, hearty and robust. Like Nehemiah, Billy is a man of joy. The joy of the Lord is his strength;[1] and the joy of the Lord brings laughter.

Is there by any chance a theology of laughter? Listen to what Paul Rader, a Chicago evangelist and ex-boxer, said on the subject:

When God chooses a man, He puts laughter into his life. God is delighted to fill the hearts of men and women with laughter. The anointing oil that was poured upon the head of David put laughter into David's life. Laughter, after all, is the surplus of life; it is a bubbling over of the emotions, a kind of spasm of exuberance, a delight of the human heart that makes the thorax cackle. It is something that warms the heart and brain and imagination so that men and women are moved to overflowing delight.[2]

Billy Graham may not "bubble over," to use Rader's expression, but from what I know of him, he shares the same view of joy. It's not the "religious" or "ceremonial" kind of joy that scholars often discuss. Such joy is usually long on solemn pronouncements and short on smiles and merriment. Billy contends that *merry* is a good Bible word. At the same time he, like all Spirit-filled believers, avoids the frantic, sensual, plastic kind of joy that the world loves. He may begin a crusade message with a light story that dissolves any "sermonic" atmosphere, but often he is actually laughing at himself.

On one occasion in 1954 he had been invited to give a fifteen-minute talk at the London School of Economics to a distinctly hostile and playful crowd of British students. As John Pollock tells the story, there were boos when Billy stood to speak.[3] He told some amusing anecdotes and was moving into his serious message when a crash of glass brought a student through an upper window, where he stood crouching with his chin and lower lip jutted out, scratching himself like an ape while the audience roared. Billy Graham looked at the young man, laughed, and said, "He reminds me of my ancestors." Everyone joined in the laughter. Then he added, "Of course, all my ancestors came from Britain." That brought down the house. When the laughter subsided, Billy gave his message, vigorous and uncompromising, to an audience in respectful silence.

One year later, after a tremendous nationwide crusade in Scotland, Graham returned to London. He had been invited to preach to Queen Elizabeth II and the Duke of Edinburgh in the Royal Chapel at Windsor Castle. When the word got out to the press, *Punch*, that incomparable British humor magazine, published some advice to the visiting American, parodying a Lewis Carroll rhyme:

> "*You are young, Dr. William!*" *the equerry cried,*
> "*with procedural problems to grapple;*
> *It may be all right to be 'Billy' outside,*
> *but NOT, if you please, in the Chapel.*"[4]

Perhaps because I was once a military chaplain, I have remembered for all these years a story Billy told at the San Francisco crusade in 1958:

"This American soldier woke up one morning in his barracks

and began behaving strangely. He walked around groping with his hands and saying, 'Where is it? Where is it?'

"His buddies, finding him ignoring their questions, tipped off the sergeant, who grilled him but got no response. All the soldier would say was, 'Where is it?' He was ordered to report to his commanding officer, whom he likewise vexed, and who in turn sent him to the hospital, where the psychiatrist examined him.

"'What's your problem, soldier?'

"'Where is it?'

"They finally decided to give him a 'Section 8' and sent him to the Post Separation Center. There he went around to the various offices, saying nothing except 'Where is it?' In time he was handed his official discharge from military service. He looked at it and exclaimed, 'There it is! That's it!'"

On another occasion I heard Billy tell about a man who was walking down a road, and behind him followed a pig. A friend who saw the man called to him, asking how he got the pig to follow him. He replied, "It's very simple. Every step I take, I drop a bean, and the pig likes beans." The point of Billy's story was that Satan goes along the road of life dropping his beans in front of people, and they follow him eagerly to their destruction. But the sight of Billy Graham stooping as he walked around the platform looking for beans and making pig noises had his audience in stitches.

Laughter has played a healthy role in Judaism and Christianity ever since Sarah laughed at finding herself pregnant. The reformers Luther and Zwingli loved to exchange humorous stories with their students and friends. Other Christian leaders who were known to enjoy a good laugh were Hugh Latimer, John Bunyan, George Whitefield, Dwight L. Moody, Samuel Porter Jones, Charles Spurgeon, and Billy Sunday.

The question as to whether Jesus ever laughed has been debated for centuries, but as far as I am concerned, there is no debate. He wept, didn't He? Billy Graham wrote in *The Secret of Happiness*, "We never read of Jesus laughing, though I am sure He did."[5] Of course He laughed. As Creator of the universe, He invented smiles and laughter. Furthermore, every person whom Jesus saves, and who is filled by the Spirit with the love of God, senses the joy and sooner or later begins to laugh—usually sooner. If he or she doesn't, something is fishy. "Jesus people" love to laugh because they are created in His image. That's how we know Jesus laughed.

Billy has also written:

One of the characteristics of the Christian is inward joy. Even under difficult circumstances, there will be a joyful heart and a radiant face. Unfortunately many Christians go around with droopy faces that give no outshining glory to God. Upon meeting a Christian, it is not hard to tell whether or not he is a victorious, spiritual, yielded believer. A true Christian should be relaxed and radiant, capable of illuminating and not depressing his surroundings. I have found in my travels that those who keep Heaven in view remain serene and cheerful on the darkest day.

In all ages people have found it possible to maintain the spirit of joy in the hour of trial. In circumstances that would have felled most people, they have so completely risen above them that they have actually used the circumstances to serve and glorify Christ.

There are times when I feel I don't have joy, and I get on my knees and say, "Lord, where is the fruit of the Spirit of joy in my life?" I find that the joy is there down deep—it is a deep river. Whatever the circumstance, there is a river of joy. In these times of upheaval and uncertainty, it is important that the trustful and forward-looking Christian remains optimistic and joyful.[6]

The Billy Graham crusades create a kind of paradox. When Billy preaches, he inveighs strongly against sin. He condemns the wicked activities of Satan. He warns about judgment and doom. He is very sober. He shakes his head and points his finger. He draws biblical pictures of hell, the abyss, and the lake of fire. He speaks of a day when God's wrath will deal with evil forever. And for many hundreds of people who do not know Christ when they come to the crusade, there is an awful chasm to face. The choices of time are binding in eternity, and they must choose. Death comes to us all, and punishment for sin is real because hell is real.

Here is the paradox. Some people come away from the stadium weeping, but these are tears of joy. They have chosen God; or rather, He has chosen them. What a relief for them that the danger of eternal judgment has been taken away! What a mercy that Jesus paid it all at the cross—for them. Tears, yes, but tears of joy.

So now the newly-forgiven can join other hundreds of believers who have come away from the stadium smiling and lighthearted. The new believers can laugh with them, for the burden of sin is lifted. They know they are redeemed and are now filled with hope. They can join in singing the songs of the redeemed.

> *Soon and very soon*
> *we're going to see the King!*

Worries about the future are gone, and they are on their way to enjoying life. They love Jesus. They claim Him as their Savior and Lord. They are therefore free to join the merry atmosphere of heaven-bound pilgrims who are, or should be, jubilant and full of fun.

Such is what Jesus intended His church to be like.

Well, why not? Those who have crossed the bridge have moved to God's side of the street; and that's where Billy lives. When he leaves the pulpit, he is in prayer and thanksgiving to God, and he leaves the scowlers on the other side.

Billy worked his humor on me once. He paid a visit to his Minneapolis headquarters and came up to the third floor and into my little office. When he comes to his main office, he does so at odd hours to avoid disturbing the staff. I happened to be absent. Billy left a note on my desk that read: "Dear Woody, I was here to see you, but you were not here. You do a good job. God bless you. Billy." Immediately I began to feel guilty until I noted the time of his visit: Sunday at 3 P.M.!

A few months later he came by my office again after business hours and left another note: "Dear Woody, Came to see you, and for the second time I find you away from your desk. Just said a prayer for you. Billy."

That's my boss!

Another time in 1963 when we were in Paris for a crusade, I left the Californian Hotel and was walking to the Champs Elysées to post

a letter. Suddenly I heard my name called. I looked around; no pedestrians were on the street, and no cars were in sight.

I heard the voice again: "Woody!"

At last I looked up, and just across the street, five stories above me, there was Billy Graham leaning from a balcony of a white French rococo-style building and waving at me.

"What are you doing?" I shouted back.

"Oh, I'm suffering up here," he said smiling. "How are you?"

I remember laughing and walking on toward the Champs Elysées with a warm glow in my heart.

Often my encounters with Billy have been like that—unexpected and delightful. In 1992 he came to Portland, Oregon, for a spiritual crusade that literally had the whole state aroused and millions of people praying. At a reception for Billy in a large hotel in Portland, I arrived with five ministers from our San Diego church, Horizon Christian Fellowship, including the senior pastor, Mike MacIntosh. When we walked in, people were moving to the right side of the room apparently to form a line. Our party slipped up to the front of the room on the left side. Billy had newly arrived, and the receiving line was just being organized.

When he spotted me, Billy's face broke into a smile. Time had passed since we had seen each other. I promptly walked up and received a hug, and my colleagues followed. Billy greeted Mike, and I introduced the others. By this time the line was functioning, and we quickly stepped aside. To our astonishment, the people who greeted Billy came by in large numbers and shook hands with us heartily as if we were part of the reception. It became pretty hilarious until we apologetically backed away.

Once I played golf with Billy. Believe me, that was another comical experience, I being the Prince of Duffers. I had just been to New Zealand on an errand for him, and he wanted to hear about it, so he invited me to where he was staying. The location was near a golf course in Pauma Valley at the foot of Mount Palomar in southern California.

Our foursome consisted of Billy, his Special Assistant T. W. Wilson, myself, and the club pro. Billy paired off with me. Imagine! My drive off the first tee was a good one and brought a "Whooee!" from Billy. Unfortunately he never said it again. My game sank to a point where I gave up trying and simply went for survival.

As for Billy, he kept telling me that he was having difficulty with his shots. "I can't play this kind of lie," he would say. But even his bad drives were better than my good ones. (Billy is often quoted as saying, "God answers my prayers everywhere except on the golf course.") When we finished our eighteen holes, it turned out he had scored an 83 and I was over 100. What the other scores were I have forgotten, but as for Billy's "difficulty with his shots," I got the message real good.

In 1996 Billy said on the *Larry King Live* television program that he gets his joy after preaching the Gospel not so much from people coming forward at his meetings, as from the thankful feeling that he has been obedient to God in delivering the message committed to him.

Yet the fact remains that Billy Graham enjoys people, all kinds of people, and loves to be with them. A journalist friend of mine, Arthur Matthews, wrote a graphic description of a stroll Billy took through the streets of Cleveland, Ohio, with a Salvation Army officer at the beginning of his crusade there. Arthur has given me permission to quote.

> Our tour covered the East Side community that was torn by riots six years ago. Signs of devastation were still apparent (hundreds of vacant buildings), but there were evidences of resurgence as well. Mr. Graham stopped to admire the painting job of a father home from work, then complimented an elderly couple on the garden in their front yard. He congratulated a college student on a trophy he recently won at school. In each home he visited, he prayed with his hosts.
>
> Few young people were in evidence on the streets, but we found plenty of them inside the Salvation Army Multi-Purpose Center, which has become a symbol of the area's hope. This morning its pool proved a popular spot; Mr. Graham grasped many wet, outstretched hands.
>
> Later he watched children playing table tennis and bumper pool, then joined some boys shooting baskets in the gymnasium. Others he saw roller-skating to lively music. In an art class he inspected craft work and encouraged some of the youngsters. In another part of the center he saw how the needs of unwed mothers are being met (some are under twelve years of age). He toured the prenatal clinic and a school where nutrition, sewing, and other courses are taught.
>
> We then drove across town to the West Side market, arriving just before noon. We found a variety of first- and second-generation Americans in this cosmopolitan area. More Hungarians live here than in any other place outside Hungary. The market's aisles were crowded as we went from stall to stall, examining the offerings of chitterlings and cheese and chickens.
>
> Our tour was unannounced, but some of those in the crowd with whom he rubbed shoulders recognized Mr. Graham. A janitor wheeled his trash container up and down the aisles, broadly grinning as he announced the visitor's

presence. "Welcome to Cleveland," said a young lady. "God bless you," said another. At one counter the evangelist was presented with a gift of exotic cheese; at another, with some ham imported from Germany's Black Forest.

As he reached the street exit, Mr. Graham opened the door for a hesitating woman. She paused outside on the sidewalk, and after the introductions, she told him with a smile, "Mr. Graham, I am legally blind, but God has given me spiritual sight. I pray for you every day."[7]

The stories about Billy Graham's personal effect on people—tens of thousands of people, even those who have not heard him preach—are endless. In one American city a Roman Catholic woman told a member of the Graham team that she had asked her priest what his advice would be as to attending a crusade meeting. "My advice," he had said, "would be not to attend."

Making a splash: Billy pauses on a city tour to chat with young swimmers at a neighborhood center during his crusade in Cleveland in 1972.

"I am sorry," she said, "but I think I'm going anyway."

The priest replied, "So am I."[8]

Finally, let me relate what happened at a team meeting in Chicago in July 1975 when I was *not* present. Billy, as I was told later, was giving a current update to the team on all the manifold activities of the Billy Graham Evangelistic Association. At one point he said, "And now we come to *Decision* magazine and Woody. Let me tell you about Woody. If I were going to send out an evangelist, I wouldn't send out Woody." Then he added something like, "But every time he goes out to preach, God uses him in surprising ways."

Remember my fruitless evangelistic efforts in the pulpit in South Dakota? If there was a difference in my preaching between 1958 and 1974, it was entirely the work of the Holy Spirit, thanks to something that happened in 1972. I will say no more about it here except that after that experience, when I was invited out to preach, I began extending invitations at the close of my messages.

But what did Billy hear that caused him to make such a statement? I believe one of the ministers from Norfolk, Virginia, was talking to Billy and had mentioned me. Billy had recently preached in Norfolk during his Tidewater Virginia crusade, which embraced Norfolk, Hampton, Portsmouth, and Newport News. On Sunday morning during the crusade, I was invited by the pastor of the First Presbyterian Church of Norfolk, Rev. H. L. Wilson, to preach in his pulpit. I remember the church well, for the building was a magnificent edifice. So I preached to Pastor Wilson's congregation and gave an invitation. A number of people came down to the altar where I led them in prayer.

What Mr. Wilson told Billy Graham afterward, so I heard, was that it was the first time in 200 years that a preacher had given an invitation in that pulpit and people had responded by walking down to the front of the church to meet God.

But wait. Wasn't that the one who . . .

Now you understand something special about Billy. He would agree with Dean Inge of St. Paul's, London, who said, "I have never understood why it should be considered derogatory to the Creator to suppose that He has a sense of humor."[9]

THE HARVEST

~

Twenty-Five

THE INTERNATIONAL CONGRESSES

~

HE WILL TEACH US HIS WAYS,
AND WE SHALL WALK IN HIS PATHS.

—ISAIAH 2:3

As editor of Billy's magazine *Decision* and later as editor emeritus, I with others on the team attended all the wonderful congresses: Berlin, 1966; Lausanne, 1974; and Amsterdam, 1983 and 1986. We saw God's children coming together from every nook and cranny of the planet—people of nearly every nation, race, color, and language; some well-to-do, many in poverty, but all in love with their Lord and eager to learn more from Him and about Him.

It is hard to realize that all these gatherings—and there were many besides, some of which I attended—took place in the mind of one man before they materialized into the reality of tens of thousands of people coming from around the globe. Billy Graham held no office, was elected by no one, possessed no authority, offered no inducement, and yet they came eagerly at his bidding to prepare themselves better for the tasks to which they were called.

Whatever skills God gave me as a writer are stretched beyond capacity when I attempt to describe what transpired at these congresses. One thing is clear: In the four meetings over a period of twenty years, Billy Graham was seeking to bring together in fellowship those deeply interested in and committed to evangelism in the name of Christ (Berlin, West Germany); then those who were actually engaging in the work of evangelism wherever they might be (Lausanne, Switzerland); and finally those who, like himself (and like Jesus), were itinerant evangelists traveling from place to place for the purpose of spreading the Gospel of salvation (Amsterdam I and II, The Netherlands).

Since my treatment of the congresses cannot be comprehensive, it must necessarily be subjective. From the four major congresses I have chosen certain elements that spoke to my own spirit and will, I hope, convey some impression of what happened.[1] It doesn't seem as if there will ever be anything quite like them again, so free were they of theological argument and ecclesiastical politics.

BERLIN, 1966

The World Congress on Evangelism

"God finally got hold of a church meeting." That is the way my report in *Decision* magazine described the World Congress on Evangelism held in the Kongresshalle of West Berlin October 25 to November 4, 1966.

Called by Billy Graham, the congress was sponsored by *Christianity Today* magazine (which he founded) as a tenth birthday celebration. Editor Carl F. H. Henry, Dr. Victor B. Nelson, and Rev. Stanley Mooneyham coordinated the event. It was the first such congress of, by, and for Bible-believing evangelicals ever to be held in 2,000 years of church history. Billy suggested that it might be compared in some ways with the Jerusalem Council, which was presided over by James, the brother of the Lord, and recorded in Acts 15:6-29.

Adding significance to the event was the fact that an ugly wall surrounded West Berlin, and Communist guards shot everyone attempting to ride past "Checkpoint Charlie" or otherwise breach the manned borders that hemmed in the city on all sides.

Before the congress began, a full-dress Billy Graham crusade was conducted in the Berlin Deutschlandhalle for six days, attended by 90,000 people. An incident took place in one of those meetings that is remarkable for what it tells about Billy Graham. Remember that

Royal entrance: His Highness, Emperor Haile Selassie of Ethiopia (right center) and Lutheran Bishop Otto Dibelius of Berlin-Brandenburg lead the procession at the beginning of the 1966 World Congress on Evangelism in West Berlin. With them are General Director Carl F. H. Henry (left) and Rev. Billy Graham.

Germany had known Christianity since the early years of the Christian era, and German Christians are not always impressed by some of our more assertive American soul-winners. But I was there and heard and saw this.

Lutheran Bishop Otto Dibelius, courageous foe of Hitler and retired bishop of Berlin-Brandenburg, sat in the audience at the crusade. Two evenings later Billy invited him to address the gathering. The bishop (who died soon after the crusade and congress ended) stepped to the podium and addressed Billy with a smile: "You said when I sat in the crowd the other evening that you would change places with me. Now I take you at your word."

He then made the following statement:

A Communist poet in Berlin named Bertolt Brecht wrote twenty years ago, "Wake up, you complacent and rutty Christians!" Now perhaps I am in a rut. However, I refuse to accept such criticism from a man who is not a Christian and does not want to become a Christian. That does not mean I will not accept it from someone else.

The Gospel is first of all judgment; grace comes afterward. So I will accept the message, "Wake up!" from one who says that I have already faced the judgment and have passed it, and who recognizes that I have now arrived at a very joyous kind of Christian faith and life.

This other person, then, from whom I will accept such a message is Billy Graham. And during this past week such an awakening has been experienced by many of us. Many, too, have made a very real decision here. This Christian decision is most important for our youth.

The whole world needs to be told about Jesus Christ. But what shall we do with a generation that likes to hear and to discuss and then make no decision at all? What is needed particularly in Berlin today are men and women who will step forward and decide for Christ. It seldom happens here; but it has happened this week.

That statement is pure gold.

In the following week the congress opened, and two highly unusual events took place that had nothing to do with "vopos" at the Brandenburg Gate, Communist politics, or the Cold War. The first was the appearance of a genuine Christian ruler. We were introduced to His Imperial Majesty, the reigning Emperor of Ethiopia, Haile Selassie I. Following is a segment of the address which His Royal Highness delivered in person to the 900 delegates from around the world, plus the 300 observers and 170 members of the press:

Jesus Christ has said, "Where two or three are gathered together in my name, there am I in the midst of them." It is therefore our expressed hope that these words will be realized in their full significance in this great assembly. We are happy to be present in this famous city of Berlin. We thank Mr. Billy Graham for inviting us to address this meeting.

We learn from the Holy Scriptures that the first Ethiopian who confessed faith in Jesus Christ was baptized only a few months after the death and resurrection of our Lord. From then on Christianity spread steadily among the Ethiopian people and became the religion of the Ethiopians in the fourth century A.D.

In these modern days there are a multitude of things published and broadcast. Many new ideas are disseminated, and wonderful appliances are produced to make life more comfortable. The rich powers are vying with each other to explore and conquer the moon and the planets. Knowledge is increasing in a bewildering manner. All this is good and praiseworthy, but what will be the end of it all? It is our firm belief that only what the Lord wills will be done. Man makes himself and his wisdom the beginning and end of his aim in life, and we are convinced that the end of this is destruction and death.

All the activities of the children of men not guided by the Spirit and counsel of God will bear no lasting fruit and will not be acceptable in the sight of the Lord and will come to nought as did the Tower of Babel. For this reason Christian leaders have an enormous responsibility. Oh, Christians, let us arise and with the spiritual zeal and earnestness which characterized the apostles and early Christians, let us labor to lead our brothers and sisters to our Savior Jesus Christ who only can give life in its fullest sense.

The second spectacular event was the testimony of two converted spear hunters out of the Stone Age. These Auca Indian converts from South America had been dressed in European clothes and brought to Berlin by an American missionary. One of them, Yaeti Kimo, had taken part in the tragic slaughter of five young American missionaries in the Curaray River deep in the jungles of eastern Ecuador ten years earlier on January 6, 1956. The appearance of these two tribes-men created a sensation at the congress. They were the fruit of American missionary efforts among a savage people.

The missionary who accompanied them to Berlin was Rachel Saint, sister of Nate Saint, one of the five martyrs. As I wrote in *Decision* at the time, "Scarcely a delegate was not stirred to his roots as he listened to Yaeti Kimo and Komi Gikita, members of the dreaded Auca tribe of Ecuador, describe in clear, vivid language the change that Jesus had wrought in their hearts."

When I asked Kimo to "tell us where you live," he replied, "I live in Tiwaeno, and I came here to speak for God and go home." We stared at the two savage Indians, tamed by a power beyond the natural man's ability to fathom, as they spoke in solemn church assembly and declared the Lord Jesus and His love. At the close of their testimonies, joy erupted as one African delegate leaped onto the stage and hugged the two Indian visitors.

LAUSANNE, 1974

The International Congress on World Evangelization

This congress was called by Billy Graham to bring together from around the globe persons actually engaged in evangelistic work, whether pastors, lay persons, or traveling evangelists. It met in the Palais de Beaulieu in Lausanne, Switzerland, from July 16 to 25, 1974.

From the very beginning Billy ruled out the perennial tendency of church gatherings to concentrate on world miseries and then spend the precious days debating the "social implications of the Gospel." He quoted Robert E. Speer, a distinguished missionary statesman of the past generation: "It is a dangerous thing to charge ourselves openly before the world with the aim of reorganizing states and reconstructing society. Missions are powerful . . . because they ignore the face of society and deal with it at its heart."

For a few days Lausanne became a global village of love at a time when the Cold War was waxing in intensity. The distinguished Swiss

Reformed church leader, Georges-Andre Chavallaz, who welcomed the delegates, spoke of the current "diplomatic colloquies" that were "nothing less than elegant dances with the polite purpose of deferring the brutal shock which is stubbornly approaching." The "brutal shock" was the outbreak of nuclear war.

I wrote these words at the time:

What was Lausanne '74? It was a *catalyst*. What the Christian leaders learned about winning people to Christ, they were to take home in order to train others. The pooling of information was not just for training the participants; it was for the mobilizing of the whole church to evangelize.

It was a *potato masher*. The phrase was used by Juan Carlos Ortiz of Buenos Aires, and I quote from his speech: "We are like potatoes. Potatoes when they are planted are grouped by two, three, or four in each plant. Then comes the harvest; they take the potatoes and put all of them in one box. But that is not unity yet; that's only regrouping. That's only confraternity and fellowship, but not unity. Those potatoes have to be peeled. When they are peeled and put together, they say, 'Ah, now we are one.' Not yet. They must be cut. Because cut ones become mashed potatoes. Hallelujah! Not many potatoes but one mashed potato!

"When the potatoes are mashed, not one of the potatoes can say, 'Ah, this is me!' And that is what the Holy Spirit— Hallelujah!—is starting to do today. Love is the key to world evangelization."

Lausanne was also *a global village*. Never before had so many individuals from so many evangelical churches, nations, and language groups gathered together. Among them were Korean missionaries to Thailand, Japanese missionaries to Indonesia, and African missionaries to the United States.

It was a *watershed*. The Lausanne Covenant affirmed among other things the participants' belief in the "divine inspiration, truthfulness and authority of the Scriptures in their entirety." Signing was voluntary but virtually unanimous.

It was an *altar*. At the deeply moving closing service at the Lord's Table, centered as it was on the cross of Christ, the congress became for precious moments a devout, worshiping world community. As Bishop Silvanus Goi Wani of East Africa expressed it: "This congress is a kind of preparation for God to meet His people here on earth before He meets them in heaven."

The congress drew 4,051 delegates from 150 nations, half of whom had come from the Third World countries. It closed with the signing of the Lausanne Covenant, committing the evangelists afresh to the worldwide task of spreading the Gospel and winning men and women to Christ.

AMSTERDAM I, 1983

The International Conference for Itinerant Evangelists

Its abbreviated name was ICIE, and it was a congress that came close to matching Dr. Graham's dreams for bringing together from around the world evangelists who travel from place to place—either from village to village or continent to continent. As Leighton Ford, associate evangelist and program director, expressed it: "This conference grew out of the heart of Billy Graham."

Nothing like it had ever been held. In 1983, some 4,000 carefully chosen itinerant evangelists gathered at the RAI Conference Center auditorium in Amsterdam, The Netherlands, for ten days, July 12-21. Many, if not most, of those who came were unrecognized, the unknown servants of the Lord who preach in cities and towns in Third World countries like Guatemala and Tanzania and Sri Lanka and in Palestinian refugee camps.

To convey the tone of the conference, I have selected a few excerpts from the talks given during the week. The first is from Billy Graham's message "The Evangelist's Plea for Decision":

The call for decision—the invitation—is not something just added to the end of an evangelistic sermon as an afterthought.

Banners of love: Flags from 133 nations in procession as the Continental Orchestra plays "Praise Ye the Lord, the Almighty" at the great gathering of itinerant evangelists in 1983.

The whole sermon leads toward it. . . . Every time I give an invitation, I am in an attitude of prayer inwardly, because I know I am totally dependent on God. This is the moment when I feel emotionally, physically, and spiritually drained. It is the part of the service that often exhausts me physically. I think one of the reasons may be the terrible spiritual battle going on in the hearts of so many people. With me it becomes such a spiritual battle that sometimes I feel almost faint. There is an inward groaning and agonizing in prayer that I cannot possibly put into words.

Rev. Tom Houston, originally of Scotland, spoke on "The Evangelist's Task of Communication." He said:

The Gospels often describe the body language of Jesus. He stretched out His hand and touched the leper. . . . He expressed surprise at the Roman officer who showed faith in Him. . . . He touched the eyes of the blind. . . . Often it was a look, as it was with the rich young ruler, and Peter when he denied Him. He looked to heaven before giving thanks to

God. . . . He bent over, He wept, He placed His hands on children, He knelt. He washed and dried His disciples' feet with a towel. For communication to be successful, the hearer must trust the speaker. The way we stand and sit, our facial expressions, the way we use our hands, are all conveying the real, inner person and increasing or decreasing trust.

The late Dr. J. Edwin Orr, distinguished historian of revivals in the life of the church, gave some discriminating counsel in his discussion of "what evangelists can do about revival." He said:

Evangelism is not revival. Popular use of the word *revival* to describe a purely evangelistic effort borders upon the ridiculous. A sign in California's San Fernando Valley announced: "Revival Every Monday!" Five miles away in Burbank another sign proclaimed: "Revival every night except Monday." The revival of the church and the awakening of the masses is the result of the outpouring of the Spirit upon the whole body of Christ, which is exclusively the work of God.

Mildred Dienert, a longtime member of the Graham team who served as prayer director for Amsterdam I, told a charming story of the way in which a busy woman found time to pray:

A great-aunt of mine who lived on Long Island, New York, had a neighbor with fourteen children. My great-aunt had no children. She would bake loaves of bread and take fruit off her trees for this family. One day she said to the mother, "I admire your gentle, quiet, loving, joyous attitude. You must be a spiritual person."

The mother smiled and said, "I do love the Lord. He's special to me."

My great-aunt said, "That's wonderful, but with all this confusion you mustn't get much time to be with Him."

The mother laughed and said, "I have a secret. You notice I wear a big apron. When I want to come apart with the Lord, I just flip the apron over my head, and the noise and chatter stops. The children all know that Mother is having her quiet time. I talk to the Lord and have Him renew my strength and revive my spirit."

Dr. Walter Smyth and Rev. Werner Burklin served as chairman and director of the ICIE. Dr. Roger Palms, editor of *Decision* magazine at that time, published a splendid special report of Amsterdam I in his November 1983 issue. During the closing Communion service the participants read together the "Amsterdam Affirmations," which provided ongoing motivation in Christ for those attending.

AMSTERDAM II, 1986

*Second International Conference
for Itinerant Evangelists*

The last of the congresses turned out to be the greatest. As the Continental Orchestra struck the notes of "All Hail the Pow'r of Jesus' Name," six torchbearers came into the Europahal at the RAI Conference Center in Amsterdam on July 12, 1986. It was an awesome moment. Representing the six continents, these men fused their flames to signify the Light of the World. At the same time 8,160 evangelists, 1,900 workers, teachers, stewards, and technicians from 174 nations and territories sang the mighty words, " . . . To Him all majesty ascribe, and crown Him Lord of all!"

Credit for this magnificent meeting goes to planners Dr. Walter Smyth, Rev. Werner Burklin, Dr. John Corts, and Rev. Robert Williams. But looking back after more than a decade, I see it now as the shadow of a man who passed by. The shadow is observable elsewhere, but during those eight days its spiritual effect on the participants was unmistakable.

What led Billy Graham to undertake these four great congresses in the twenty years from 1966 to 1986? What manner of commission did he receive from God? Were they truly human expressions of divine love? I can't answer such questions, but when I asked a fellow team member, Charlie Riggs, to say something on the subject, he simply pointed to the results.

What Mr. Graham did at the World Congress in Berlin was to start a *networking* of Christian leaders and organizations. Then came Lausanne in Switzerland, and plans were laid to reach the world with evangelism. The Lausanne Committee was formed, and thirty years later Lausanne committees are still at work around the world in evangelism.

In 1983 Mr. Graham brought together 4,000 itinerant evangelists in Amsterdam, Holland, to equip and encourage their ministries. It was so successful, and demands for a repeat were so pressing that he invited 8,000 more who had missed Amsterdam I to the same location in 1986. This networking was what led to the Global Mission ministry.

For us on the team the love motive in all this labor is unquestioned. We know, however, that the questions may be raised afresh in century twenty-one by a "generation that knows not Billy." We who have known and loved him need to have sound answers to hand on to future generations, since it is not only Billy's, but our own ministries that are involved.

Therefore I want to share with you excerpts from a well-received talk given at Amsterdam II. The speaker was Billy Kim, a prominent Korean pastor who served as interpreter for Billy Graham during his record-breaking 1973 crusade in Seoul. Whether Dr. Kim's view of revival is the same as Dr. Edwin Orr's is for you, the reader, to decide. Here in part is what Billy Kim told the delegates in 1986:

> Many people ask me why the Korean church is experiencing revival today. In the last decade, hundreds of thousands of people have come to Christ. What is the explanation? Every Christian wants to know.
>
> In 1955 there were only 4,000 churches in Korea and only one million Christians. In 1985 the census showed that Korea had 32,000 churches with nearly ten million Christians. We are building 15 new churches every day in Korea. The population of South Korea is only forty million people.
>
> I have pondered the possible reasons for this present-day revival among the people of my country. You will find more prayer meetings in the Korean church than (pardon my expres-

sion) a dog has fleas! We start at 4:30 every morning—not only in my church, but in *all* the churches. At 4:30 every morning there is a prayer meeting, winter or summer, rain or shine. I don't know who started it, but I would like to meet him.

Sometimes I have wondered why God called me back to Korea to be a pastor. It's hard to get up at four o'clock in the morning! But I wish you could see some of those early morning prayer meetings—they pray for hours! They pound on the floor, crying out to God. No wonder God is blessing the Korean church today!

Every Friday night there is an all-night prayer meeting. They have prayer and fasting meetings, 40-day prayer meetings, 100-day prayer meetings. They have more titles for prayer meetings than anything in the church program. I don't know why they have so much to pray about!

I wish you could hear some of their prayers. They pray for the unification of Korea so their families can be reunited. They pray for their pastors, for their church to have a revival. They pray for world revival, and they pray for you evangelists; and I know God answers their prayers!

I have a friend for whom we coined the name of "Hallelujah Choi." He built and owns the tallest building in the city of Seoul—sixty-three stories. He founded the first professional soccer team in Korea and named it Hallelujah. That team played in Hong Kong against the People's Republic of China; can't you hear the television commentator saying, "Hallelujah's driving the ball into left field," and "Hallelujah scored a goal! Hallelujah!"

We Korean people like that word so much. One man built a church and called it The Hallelujah Church. We have a Hallelujah Beauty Shop and a Hallelujah Supermarket. I asked the manager of The Hallelujah Restaurant, "Are you a Christian?" He said, "Sure, hallelujah!"

Let me add a personal word to what Billy Kim said back in 1986. In 1973 I was in Korea with Billy Graham, and one morning I rose at four o'clock. In company with Dr. Walter Smyth of the team, I rode in a taxi through the dark, empty streets of Seoul looking for one of those prayer meetings. Our directions were not clear, but finally we spied a woman hurrying across a street. By following her, we found the church and the people inside singing heartily. Billy Kim's description of what we saw and heard there proved to be accurate. He told it as it was.

To God be the glory!

Persons wishing further information about the messages given at these four international congresses may apply to World Wide Publications, 1313 Hennepin Avenue, Minneapolis, Minnesota 55403.

Twenty-Six

THAWING THE
COLD WAR

~

YOU WILL BE BROUGHT BEFORE RULERS AND KINGS
FOR MY SAKE, FOR A TESTIMONY TO THEM.

—MARK 13:9

Ever since Joseph told his brothers in Egypt, "You meant evil against me, but God meant it for good,"[1] we have known that the Creator of the universe sometimes takes a hand in writing history according to His own pleasure. Billy Graham learned that lesson when he accepted an invitation to speak in Russia, but it wasn't much fun.

Billy became the object of the severest and most intense criticism in the American press and media because of his visit to the Soviet Union in 1982. William F. Buckley, Jr., wrote, "Billy, won't you please come home?" The Chicago *Tribune* ended a discussion of "Billy Graham and Pig-Wrestling" with the comment: "Never wrestle with a pig; you'll both get dirty, and the pig likes it." Many critical editorials appeared, but I quote from only one, in *The San Diego Union*, May 14, 1982:

> Dr. Graham has permitted his good name and his ministry to be exploited for the benefit of Soviet propaganda. It was bad enough that Dr. Graham lent his name and presence to the Soviet-sponsored "Worldwide Conference of Religious Workers for Saving the Sacred Gift of Life from Nuclear Catastrophe." This affair was never destined to be anything

more than a thoroughly manipulated component of the Soviet Union's patently duplicitous "peace offensive." Its purpose . . . is to weaken Western defenses.

But the real shocker came in the form of statements from Dr. Graham suggesting that he had no quarrel with the Soviet Union's record on matters of religious freedom. . . . The political and, yes, moral price he is being made to pay is much, much too high.

Similar criticisms and attacks came from all across America. Some were unbelievably hostile. The cavilers seemed to take pleasure in rebuking a man who had hitherto been held up as a model of exemplary behavior and good citizenship. Protesters paraded in front of the Billy Graham Center in Wheaton, Illinois, carrying signs that read, "Billy Graham has been duped by the Soviets" and "Graham eats caviar as Russian Christians suffer in jails." *The New York Times* said, "Heaven only knows what Mr. Graham wanted to accomplish with his misguided denials of Soviet repression." Claims were made that even Russian Christians were "numbed and shocked by Graham's apparent lack of sensitivity to the persecuted." Dan Rather, the CBS newscaster, declared that Billy "was *had*—deceived and used."[2]

After having read Billy Graham's remarks made at the World Peace Conference that drew this criticism, together with his explanation of those remarks, I can understand why Billy himself was shocked at the outburst of hostility that met him on his return to London from Moscow.

Far back in the Eisenhower years when Senator McCarthy was accusing the State Department of being riddled with Communists, Billy Graham first sensed God's call to preach the Gospel behind the Iron Curtain. In 1959 we on the Graham team knew that he was making a quick trip to Moscow on a tourist visa. While there he met secretly with half a dozen Christians, knelt in Red Square and prayed, and then visited the empty Lenin Stadium, where a photo was taken of him in the bleachers praying.

In 1977, after five years of difficult negotiations with Communist officials (skillfully handled by Billy's friend Alexander Haraszti and BGEA team members Walter Smyth and John Akers), the Iron Curtain cracked a bit. Graham paid a ten-day restricted visit to Hungary at the hesitant invitation of the Communist government. The response of the Hungarian people to his gospel message was beyond all expectation in a dictatorship. Wherever the crowds gathered, people started calling, "Billee! Billee!" A year later, in October 1978, when Billy paid a similar visit to Poland, it was with equally exciting and fruitful results.

During the Hungarian visit Billy opened preliminary negotiations with Soviet Baptist leaders with a view to his long-prayed-for trip to Russia. Later in Washington, D.C., Billy met with Soviet Ambassador Anatoly Dobrynin and Metropolitan Philaret of the Russian Orthodox church. Further plans were interrupted when Leonid Brezhnev made his Christmas decision to invade Afghanistan with Soviet troops, and President Jimmy Carter responded by withdrawing American participation in the 1980 Moscow Olympic Games.

It was apparent during the early 1980s that the atheistic grip on Eastern Europe was gradually and quietly loosening. A motion picture produced in Soviet Georgia, *Repentance,* had a religious message at its core. It held that the church had been destroyed, and without it there could be no basis for civilized society. Eighty percent of Russians, it was estimated, viewed that film.

Certainly the old days of Lenin and Stalin and Khrushchev were gone. But atheism was still in force, and the KGB was still all-powerful; and as Dr. John Akers has pointed out, Billy Graham was virtually alone among Western church leaders in having any access to East European leadership.

It was at this time (1982) that Patriarch Pimen, head of the Russian Orthodox church, issued his call for a peace conference of world religious leaders to oppose the threat of nuclear war. Despite the church sponsorship, the conference was obviously a Soviet Communist propaganda effort. Soviet leaders were aware that Billy Graham's presence would add prestige to their conference.

During negotiations with Metropolitan Philaret over Billy

Graham's participation, Dr. Haraszti made a sensational statement that is recorded in William Martin's biography:

> I don't compare Dr. Graham with the patriarch or the pope, because Dr. Graham is not the head of a church. He is the head of all Christianity . . . in a spiritual way. The pope cannot preach to all the Protestants, but Billy Graham can preach to all the Roman Catholics. The patriarch cannot preach to all the Roman Catholics; they will not listen to him. But Billy Graham can preach to all the Orthodox, and they will listen to him, because he is above these religious strifes. He is a man of higher stature. . . .

My purpose at the moment is not to inquire as to whether Billy should or should not have appeared and spoken in Moscow at the Communist-sponsored world conference of Religious Workers for Saving the Sacred Gift of Life from Nuclear Catastrophe. Instead, I will give my opinion of the speech Billy made there, which I have read. Of all the sermons and addresses I have ever heard by Billy Graham or read in print over a period of forty years, his speech delivered on May 11, 1982, at that "peace conference" was to me his finest.

It was titled "The Christian Faith and Peace in a Nuclear Age," and it stamped Billy not only as a committed Christian but as a lover of peace and a world statesman of quality.[3] In my judgment it outdistances the anti-nuclear utterances I have read that keep emerging from both the United Nations Organization and the World Council of Churches.

The real significance of Billy's visit to Moscow in 1982 can best be understood from the perspective of later developments. He worshiped in Baptist and Russian Orthodox churches and made friends with many Christian leaders. In the years that followed he was invited to preach in East Germany, Czechoslovakia, and Romania. In 1984 he returned by invitation to the Soviet Union, and this time he spoke fifty times in four cities: Moscow, Leningrad, Tallinn, and Novosibirsk. He met with government and Christian leaders and was used of God to lead thousands of Russians into the kingdom of God.

Meanwhile astonishing changes were taking place in the leadership of the Soviet government. Brezhnev died in 1982 and was succeeded briefly as general secretary by Andropov and then by Chernenko. By early 1985 both men were dead of natural causes, and in March Mikhail Gorbachev took over the seat of government.

Gorbachev soon embarked on new Soviet policies of *perestroika* (restructuring) and *glasnost* (openness), which together opened the door to many new attitudes in his administration. Although Gorbachev himself remained a convinced Marxist, he lifted the ban on religious activity for the first time in seven decades and gave great encouragement to the leaders of the churches.

President Ronald Reagan held summit meetings with Gorbachev, and in 1988 he invited the Soviet leader to Washington, D.C. Billy Graham was the only clergyman present at Gorbachev's arrival, and later he became an invited guest at the state dinner held in Gorbachev's honor at the White House. In the following year, to the amazement of the whole world, the Berlin Wall was demolished, and the Soviet Union broke up after seventy-two years of tyranny.

In October 1992, God answered the prayer Billy had offered back in 1959. He was invited to conduct a three-day evangelistic crusade in Moscow. It was held not in Lenin Stadium, but in the Olympic Stadium, which twelve years earlier had been the site of the Olympic Games that the United States had boycotted.

Joining in the invitation originally extended by Patriarch Pimen were Russian Orthodox, Baptist, Pentecostal, Lutheran, and Adventist churches, 150 in Moscow and 3,000 in the surrounding country.

What a crusade! Each night eager Muscovites filled the 38,000-seat stadium to hear Billy. On the first evening inquirers coming forward signed 10,641 cards of commitment; on the second evening 12,628 signed. On the closing Sunday afternoon 50,000 persons had jammed into the stadium. Another 30,000 stood outside where a huge television screen with audio echoed what was happening. The number of cards signed was 19,417.

As one reflects on the momentous historical changes in the closing years of the twentieth century, it is difficult to assess Billy Graham's actual involvement in those changes. Rather than dispute the distribution of credits, I would be more interested in going back to that other question: Was Billy's visit to Moscow back in 1982 the "mistake" that the American media and much of the public took it to be?

Billy Graham has stated publicly many times in recent years that God has told him to work and pray for world peace. That was, in my opinion, the clear and undoubted motivation that sent him to the Soviet Union, and it was certainly in line with Jesus' seventh Beatitude: "Blessed are the peacemakers."[4]

As I said at the beginning of this chapter, God has a way of changing the way we look at history. "You meant it to me for evil," said Joseph to his brothers, "but God meant it to me for good."

Dan Rather of CBS, who had been one of Billy's critics, said in 1990 on television:

> Before anybody else I knew of, and more consistently than anyone I have known, of any nationality, race, or religion, Rev. Graham was saying, "Spirituality is alive in the Marxist-Leninist-Stalinist states. We may not see it very often, we may not hear it very often, we may not see or hear it at all, but it's there, and I know it's there." Frankly, there were those years when I thought he was wrong or that he didn't know what he was talking about, and it turns out he was right.[5]

Edward L. Plowman, a Christian journalist who accompanied Billy Graham on all his trips to the Soviet Union, wrote several articles stoutly defending Billy's mission and pointing out how his words had been misconstrued and misrepresented. Plowman today is convinced that Billy's ministry behind the Iron Curtain was "part of an overall plan of God."

Ken Garfield, religion editor of the Charlotte *Observer*, told me that what really demolished the Soviet Union was "the joy of faith and the desire for freedom" on the part of the Russian people. He added that "Billy Graham was a contributing factor in helping them to give expression to that joy and that desire, and was in fact one of the first to do so."

Dr. Carl F. H. Henry, founding editor of *Christianity Today*, agreed. He said to me, "From the vantage point of the ultimate collapse of the Communist empire, it is apparent that Billy Graham's ministry made a contribution at least indirectly to that collapse. In any case the Bible teaching is clear: God in His sovereignty overrules. As a Christian, you do what the Spirit tells you to do. Billy did and he went."

William Martin, author of *A Prophet with Honor: The Billy Graham Story,* told me that Russian Christians today have acknowledged to him that Billy Graham's role was helpful.[6] "Billy was the point man in Russia," Dr. Martin said. "Some mistakes were made, but instead of defending himself, he kept his mouth shut. As a result he was able in 1992 to conduct a public crusade in Moscow, which for years had been his long-term goal."

Someone once said that "God became tired of Napoleon." Perhaps the same could be said of Communist leaders. Whatever the reason, the fact is that in our own time the Cold War ended, the Berlin Wall came crashing down, the Iron Curtain lifted, and millions of people in eleven time zones are breathing freely again. Ukrainians, Estonians, Latvians, Lithuanians, Armenians, Georgians, Moldovans, Mongolians, and many others are finding a new identity and are again free to worship openly the Lord they love.

Did Billy Graham really help thaw the Cold War? Did he make a difference as he rode around Moscow in Soviet limousines with Communist officials? God knows. He keeps the books. It is now acknowledged that some of those officials were secret believers. Former President Richard Nixon said in 1990, "There's no question that he (Billy) helped bring about the peaceful liberation of Eastern Europe and some of the present opposition to communism in the Soviet Union." And about the same time President George Bush, at a National Prayer Breakfast in Washington, D.C., is reported to have said (referring to the Cold War) that Billy Graham saw what God was doing long before the politicians did.[7]

The clearest statement of the truth in this controversial matter was made to me by Richard G. Capen, Jr., former publisher of the Miami *Herald* and vice chairman of Knight-Ridder Newspapers, and more recently U.S. ambassador to Spain under President Bush. Mr. Capen is also a board member of the Billy Graham Evangelistic Association. Here is what he said:

> If the American media criticized Billy Graham for going to Moscow back in 1982, it was because they did not see what he saw or sense what he sensed. Dr. Graham was aware of a spiritual undertone in the populace of the Soviet Union that had been suppressed by a closed society. When he went to participate in the peace conference, it was because he recognized an opportunity to be a beacon of hope to the people of God in Russia.
>
> He also sensed a spark of spiritual vitality not only among the Russians, but among all the peoples of Eastern Europe. As a person of some international stature himself, he determined to fan that spark. To Billy Graham it was a God-given calling. It was definitely not a mistake to make the trip to Moscow, as the eventual collapse of the Soviet empire has proved without a doubt.
>
> In recent years Dr. Graham has undertaken a similar ministry in North Korea, where as in Russia there is a strong spiritual element in the population. His visits to Pyongyang have built a bridge that the media and the politicians have yet to cross.[8]

When Billy Graham sat in the empty Lenin Stadium back in 1959, he prayed to God that he might be allowed to come back and preach the Gospel to the Russian people. When he finally returned in 1982, he may have expected some criticism at home, but he had no idea of the beating he would take. God heard him and sent him anyway. As Joseph said to his brothers in Egypt, God meant it for good. And it was good. Thousands of the children of Mother Russia are now going to heaven.

Weeping is for a night, but joy comes in the morning.[9] My wife, Ruth, and I visited the former Soviet Union in 1996, and judging from what we saw and heard, I can believe that the memory of Billy Graham's friendship is enshrined in the hearts of millions of Christians in Russia, Belarus, Ukraine, the Baltic states, Hungary, Romania, Poland, and the other East European countries.

Twenty-Seven

INTO
ALL THE WORLD

~

WE, ACCORDING TO HIS PROMISE, LOOK FOR NEW HEAVENS
AND A NEW EARTH IN WHICH RIGHTEOUSNESS DWELLS.

—2 PETER 3:13

When will the world come to an end?

We all wonder about it. Philosophers ruminate sagely. Scientists offer knowledgeable guesses. Astrologers play with numbers. Science-fiction writers scribble off lurid descriptions. Filmmakers produce even more lurid descriptions. Comedians conjure up jokes. Preachers refer to scriptural warnings. Kids dread it.

But Christian children go to Sunday school and sing happy songs such as:

> *We are longing for His coming,*
> *we are looking to the skies,*
> *we are watching, we are waiting . . .*

Are they really singing about the end of the world?

In Matthew 24:14, Jesus says, "This gospel of the kingdom will be preached in all the world as a witness to all the nations, and then the end will come." That verse seems to answer the key question of the future, for it tells us *when*. That answer may raise eyebrows at the Hale Observatory on Mount Palomar, California, but nobody seems to be able to find a better one in the telescope.

For Billy Graham, as for many Spirit-filled evangelists for the past

2,000 years, Matthew 24:14 has been a challenge to carry the Gospel the length and breadth of our planet. Billy's whole career over half a century has been, in a sense, his response to that verse. He is convinced that Jesus Christ meant what He said, and Billy has taken it personally by making the second coming of Christ the crown and centerpiece of his closing crusade messages.

Wherever he is preaching, Billy spends his final Sunday afternoon moving past the Cross and the Resurrection to the future when Jesus has promised that He will return in glory and "the end will come." One by one Billy describes the prophetic signs of things to come, including the promises in Matthew. Of all the creative aspects of his ministry that have won him worldwide recognition, none has been more significant than his response to Jesus' clear call to evangelize.

Starting several decades ago, when he was first filling stadiums, Billy began experimenting with what he now calls "global evangelism." Back in 1970, with the rest of the team, I took part in one of his early experiments. The ultimate aim was what a beloved professor of mine called "the universal purpose of God revealed supremely in Christ." That purpose was and is to fulfill Jesus' command to go and make disciples and save souls.

Flanked by a brilliant British engineer, David Rennie, and a strong task force of technical experts, Billy set out to preach the Gospel, make disciples, and save souls in Dortmund, Germany, and *simultaneously* in thirty-five other major cities of Europe. People would gather in different places and watch and hear his message on 20 x 27-foot television screens reflecting giant Eidophor projectors, which in turn relayed electronic signals from Dortmund's huge Westfalenhalle. Those watching and listening lived as far away to the north as Tromsø, Norway, above the Arctic Circle, and to the south in Zagreb in what was then Yugoslavia.

What were some of the other cities participating in this electronic miracle called "Euro 70"? In Germany—Cologne, Munich, Berlin, Frankfurt, Hamburg, and Nuremberg; in Wales—Swansea; in Denmark—Copenhagen; in Belgium—Brussels and Antwerp; in Austria—Salzburg and Vienna; in England—Chatham; in Switzerland—Geneva; in Norway—Skien, Stavanger, and Bergen; in

The Netherlands—Hilversum; and in France—Paris. Total number attending the services in the thirty-six cities that week: 838,023.

What a challenge to this editor and his photographer trying to cover thirty-six stories at once! We made it from Minneapolis to Oslo and Kristiansand, Norway; to Dortmund; then to Vienna, Austria, and Zagreb. There you might say we ran out of petrol.

Don't get me wrong, it was an enchanting experience. I have sometimes said that to work for Billy Graham is to grab a strap, pray, and hang on. The call to discipleship was heard in Europe and answered. Large crowds in Norway were jubilant; the Viennese were warm and responsive; and in Zagreb the Roman Catholic Church of St. Marko Krizezcanin (the largest venue Dictator Tito would permit) bored a hole in its inner church wall so the television projector could flash Billy's message through to the screen. Everywhere people physically answered Billy's invitation and challenge by walking up in front of the screen and praying words of commitment. The experiment was a huge success. But as for my covering the rest of the cities, technology outclassed me.

Here is what I wrote in *Decision* (July 1970):

What shocked Europe was the touch of the Holy Spirit. He did what the technicians could not do. He caused men to weep and women to pray and children to stand tall in their faith. He broke the sophisticated reserve of student intellectuals. He tore the masks of pride from self-satisfied churchmen. He taught Europe a lesson it had almost forgotten: that the Gospel of Jesus Christ is "the power of God unto salvation to everyone who believes."

And not only that, the Spirit of God got into the legs of Europe. People (16,000 of them) did what everyone said they would never do. They walked forward from their seats in thirty-six cities to commit their lives to the Lord Jesus Christ.

Move ahead twenty-five years to 1995. Billy Graham had finished his experimental study of simultaneous gospel meetings in different parts of the world. He had conducted missions from London to all of Africa; from Hong Kong to much of Asia; from Essen, Germany, to all of Europe; and from Buenos Aires to all South America. Fully convinced that even wider evangelism could be achieved, he was about to launch his "Global Mission" using the latest high-tech skills and equipment to expand his outreach by satellite transmission to 185 nations simultaneously for three consecutive days.

The outstanding natural obstacle to world evangelism is language. In today's world English has become a far more prevalent and popular language than in the past and has in fact become the first truly global language. Yet it still cannot do the job. There are too many people, too many cultures, too many ways of speaking.

How has Billy Graham, who speaks only English, resolved the language problem? This modern marvel was accomplished in March 1995 by means of a multiplicity of satellites in outer space. Billy preached his three messages, a different one each night, from the podium of the crowded Hiram Bithorn Stadium in San Juan, Puerto Rico, March 16-18. He had assembled a battery of 117 translators, each to put his preaching into a different language for transmissions of the telecast over thirty-seven satellites.

The statistics boggle the mind. Live locations worldwide with satellite dishes numbered 2,999. The telecast thus reached crowds of people around the globe ranging from 5,000 to 60,000, with Billy speaking in English and the translators in San Juan rendering it in each case into the appropriate language. The viewers on six continents gathered in school buildings, churches, tents, auditoriums, cinemas, rented halls, stadiums, refugee camps, even hillsides and open fields—wherever there was a satellite dish. And supporting all the viewings were the accompanying prayer meetings, counselor-training sessions, and follow-up meetings—thousands of them dotting the surface of the earth.

Had anything like this taken place before in the history of the world? No. Nothing. Not the Olympic Games, not the landing on the moon.

Directing personnel and equipment for this vast operation called "Global Mission with Billy Graham" was Robert Williams of the team, who had held executive responsibilities in the 1980s at both Amsterdam world evangelism conferences.[1]

Good news by satellite: Graham holds his Bible and a microphone as he prepares to send the Word of Christ around the world by satellite from San Juan, Puerto Rico, in 1995.

Rather than capping his worldwide ministry, the extraordinary success of Billy's Global Mission outreach from Puerto Rico instead led him to pursue more and greater high-tech developments. In April 1996, Robert Williams was in charge of a second remarkable worldwide Billy Graham outreach, but with a distinct difference.

Whereas the Global Mission had been transmitted to locations equipped with satellite dishes, this new World Television Series program took the gospel message straight into private homes. Billy and his board of directors authorized negotiations for prime-time placement of a specially produced program on the major television networks of virtually every country in the world. My wife, Ruth, and I watched it in southern California.

Cooperating in this endeavor were an astonishing 1,040,000 churches in 204 countries. They arranged private meetings in the homes of their congregations. Reports coming in showed that attendance at the home meetings around the world averaged twenty-nine persons. While the televised program involved interviews and testimonies, the main thrust of this new outreach was capsuled in a strong message by Billy Graham entitled, "Starting Over."

This telecast was interpreted into over fifty languages as the program was produced. Afterward it was interpreted into many additional languages locally as people viewed the program.

The response was tremendous. Here is a sampling of the nations where Billy Graham's message of salvation came in April 1996: Angola, Jordan, Uruguay, Panama, Ukraine, Ecuador, Uganda, Sierra Leone, Seychelles, China, Taiwan, Macau, Philippines, England, Burundi, Russia, Croatia, Hungary, Spain, Belize, Namibia, South Africa, Congo, Guinea-Bissau, Argentina . . . In the United States the telecast went out from 438 stations.

Robert Williams told me that Billy Graham is frequently asked whether all this globe-circling evangelism is truly a fulfillment of Matthew 24:14. The question is sometimes put this way: "Since the Gospel of the kingdom has now been preached by satellite to the whole world, can we expect 'the end?' Will you bring it in?"

To this Billy has replied by quoting other statements of Jesus, such as Matthew 28:19: "Go and make disciples of all the nations." He tells the media that it is obvious "not every ear has yet heard the Gospel." If anything, he concedes that "perhaps what we are doing may be considered just a step on the way."

Let me try to sum up. Exactly when the angel Gabriel will blow his trumpet may not be clear, but from this global effort one thing is clear to me at least: The very fact that Billy Graham's message in April 1996 reached as many as 2.5 billion viewers (half the world's population) is far more than a tribute to an individual or a triumph of technology. *It is confirmation of the validity of the Evangel itself.* The redemption story is the authentic, unadulterated, infallible message of Holy Scripture. Otherwise few would listen.

Let the technicians take off their shoes with the rest of us, for they are standing on holy ground.[2]

In April 1996, when people gathered in three million households around the world, speaking in forty-five different languages, they did not come together to hear the speculations of the higher critics and Bible revisionists or the scoffings of the doubters and skeptics. They came to hear the truth as it is in Christ. For them the New Testament is the valid, normative expression of Christianity, and in their minds Jesus is the Way, the Truth, and the Life.

Leaving Billy Graham out of it for the moment, and leaving out also the various religious hierarchies, I draw tremendous joy from this outreach of 1996. It was apparent that hundreds of millions of members of the church universal were giving their assent and endorsement to the biblical message of God's eternal love. Billy himself was, as he has often said, simply a Western Union messenger boy delivering God's telegram to the door of humanity.

We may conclude that whoever questions or denies the teaching of the Gospels, of the apostles, the prophets, the psalmists, the historical books, the thirty-nine chapters of the Old Testament and the twenty-seven chapters of the New Testament does not share the kind of faith demonstrated that day in April 1996 by millions of believers in 204 nations around the world.

If that much can be said for Billy Graham's satellite evangelism, it is saying a lot. And the end is not yet. Looking ahead, more satellite telecasts are scheduled by Billy Graham and his colleagues at prime time in over 200 countries during the remaining years of the twentieth century.

Give a man credit. In time the churches may catch up to Billy Graham's spiritual vision of the universal purpose of God. But right now nobody else seems to have the imaginative zeal, the practical determination, the appeal, the team, the personnel, the volunteers, and the resources to engage in such a total global ministry.

Credit? Yes, but God commands the ultimate credit. The

almighty Sovereign of Abraham, Isaac, and Jacob took an unsophisticated Carolina farm boy and made him into His instrument to accomplish His desire in a world that was not ready for it. The result is that, despite an indifferent and often hostile environment, millions are now claiming Jesus Christ as Lord of their lives.

As for Morrow Graham's son and Ruth Graham's husband, many look to him the way I do, simply as "beloved Billy."

Twenty-Eight

L'ENVOI

~

LO, I AM WITH YOU ALWAYS.

—MATTHEW 28:20

Seventy-five thousand people have gathered in Charlotte's immense new Ericsson Stadium. The weather is mild on Sunday afternoon, September 29, 1996, as Cathy Wood, a team associate, leads Ruth and me over the stadium's perforated flooring. It is the closing day of Billy Graham's Carolina crusade, and Cliff Barrows and his choir are filling the air with the strains of Handel's *Messiah*.

On reaching the far side, we enter a tunnel under the stands that leads to a covered driveway. There by arrangement we wait, and in a few minutes a car arrives, and Billy Graham steps out.

Somehow he seems more fragile than the man who for seventeen years was my employer. Yet there is still the old magnetism, now with a fresh touch. To my quixotic mind he might be King David, the ancient Hebrew warrior, arriving in his iron chariot to meet with the leaders of his "mighty men." Or perhaps he is the venerable Joseph of Arimathea, bringing the precious grail of the Last Supper (as legend has it) to English soil after many hardships and presenting it to the congregation of the Glastonbury chapel. Or he could even be the evangelist George Whitefield arriving on Boston Common in defiance of the entire Harvard College faculty, ready to preach the everlasting Gospel of Christ to the colonists gathered by the thousands to hear him.

At the stadium: Billy Graham greets Ruth and Sherwood
Wirt on the closing day of his Carolina Crusade
in Charlotte, N.C., September 1996.

Now Billy is speaking to the crusade chairman and a few friends. He pauses, looks up, and utters one word: "Sherwood." If I am stirred, it is with good reason. I remember hearing Dale Carnegie say years ago, "The most beautiful sound in the world is the sound of one's own name." In due course we approach and shake hands with Billy. I mention our recent visit to one of his closest associates, Walter Smyth, now recovering from stroke in southern California. Billy says, "I miss him," and adds quietly, "just as I miss you."

That is all, but it is more than enough. We emerge from the tunnel onto the stadium floor exhilarated, and after crossing to the music of "How Great Thou Art," we find our seats. The crusade closes on a high note as over 3,000 persons respond to Billy's invitation to come to Christ. But that is not the ending; it is only the beginning. The Holy Spirit now goes to work in many a convicted heart on a September afternoon in Ericsson Stadium.

~ GRACE NOTE ~

Spirit, who from age to age
   raised up poet, seer, and sage,
pointing us beyond the shore,
   saying life is something more,
something past all human sight,
   past the everlasting night:
Spirit, whom the Savior sent
   to restore the joy He meant,
grind me with Your granite pestle,
   then make me an open vessel,
and with treasures of Your dower
   fill me with enabling power.
I would write the truth, no less,
   truth to tell and truth to bless,
of a life which, as a token
   of Your favor, You have broken,
saved, and healed, and through it spoken.

—S. E. W.

Appendix

"THE HOPE FOR AMERICA"

~

THEM THAT HONOR ME I WILL HONOR.

—1 SAMUEL 2:30

M odeled after the Graeco-Roman style, its marble-covered iron dome rising 287 feet above the dignified landscape, the United States capitol has stood for two centuries overlooking the Potomac River in the heart of the District of Columbia. This classic structure, so symbolic of the true national spirit of America, was designed by architect William Thornton and was accepted by President George Washington in 1793 to be the housing centerpiece of the United States government.

Beneath the majestic dome with its inscriptions and its balconies is the great central rotunda where American patriots of the past are honored. And there on Thursday, May 2, 1996, by action of the United States Congress, a special convocation of government figures and guests was held to honor two private citizens, Dr. and Mrs. William Franklin Graham.

House Resolution 2657 had been approved by both houses of Congress and signed into law by President Clinton on February 13. Then in May an audience of 700 members of Congress, diplomats, and spiritual dignitaries gathered to award the Congressional Gold Medal to the Grahams. General George Washington was the first recipient of that honor as commander-in-chief of the embattled

American military forces in 1776. Since then legislation to award the Gold Medal has been enacted only 113 times in the history of the republic. It is the highest honor the Congress can bestow on the nation's civilian population.

The authorizing legislation recognized Billy and Ruth Graham for "outstanding and lasting contributions to morality, racial equality, philanthropy, and religion." Speaking before the vote on the floor of the House, Representative Floyd Flake of New York had said, "This represents for us an opportunity to say to the American people and to the world that it is important for persons to make commitments with their lives that express the very best of what it means to be not only citizens of this nation, but citizens of the world. No one has done that more effectively than Billy Graham, with Mrs. Ruth Graham, who stands beside him as the first lady."

Speaking at the May 2 presentation were the vice president, the Senate majority leader and the speaker of the House of Representatives. Said Vice-President Albert Gore, "You have touched the hearts of the American family. Over the last one-half century, few individuals have left such a lasting impact on our national life. Every American president since World War II has sought Billy Graham's counsel. Republicans and Democrats alike have relied on his moral sense and used his wisdom as a compass to help guide the ship of state. This man, who once dreamed of swinging a bat in baseball's major leagues, has filled stadiums from New York to Nairobi, from Tulsa to Tokyo, preaching the Gospel and sounding the cry for human rights, enlightened race relations, and the dignity of freedom."

Said Majority Leader Robert Dole, "When the idea of awarding a Congressional Gold Medal to Dr. Graham was first raised, it received something rare in this building—unanimous approval. So too did the idea of honoring Ruth Graham, Billy's remarkable partner of fifty-three years and a distinguished communicator of God's power and peace in her own right."

House Speaker Newt Gingrich, chairman of the event, referred to Dr. Graham as "one of the great civic leaders of the twentieth century." He told the audience that the man they were honoring had preached to more people than anyone in history—that 100 million people had seen him in person and two billion had watched him on television.

Most of the Grahams' five children, nineteen grandchildren, and seven great-grandchildren were at the ceremony, together with evangelical Christian dignitaries and officials from the Southern Baptist denomination, to which Dr. Graham belongs.

Historically the Grahams were the third couple ever to be honored with the Gold Medal. After receiving the award from Speaker Gingrich and Senate President Pro Tempore Strom Thurmond, Dr. Graham addressed the assemblage on the subject, "The Hope for America." He opened with the words, "I would not be here today receiving this honor if it were not for an event that happened to me many years ago as a teenager on the outskirts of Charlotte, North Carolina. An evangelist came to our town for a series of meetings.[1] I came face to face with the fact that God loved me, Billy Graham, and had sent His Son to die for my sin. He told how Jesus rose from the dead to give us hope of eternal life."

Describing his conversion and faith in Christ, Dr. Graham said, "That simple repentance and open commitment changed my life. If we have accomplished anything at all in life since then, it has only been because of the grace and mercy of God."

The honoree then called the nation to renewal and repentance, and thanked God for America's heritage of freedom and abundant blessings. He said that the nation has many good qualities, but then asked if the first recipients of the Gold Medal award would recognize today the society they sacrificed to establish. "I fear not," he went on. "We have confused liberty with license, and we are paying the awful price. We are a society perched on the brink of self-destruction."

Quoting from Psalm 23, Graham pointed to three causes of current national woes endemic in society : emptiness, guilt, and the fear of death "which haunts our souls." He said, "I believe the fundamental crisis of our time is a crisis of the spirit. We have lost sight of the moral and spiritual principles on which this nation was established—principles drawn largely from the Judeo-Christian tradition found in the Bible.

"As we face a new millennium, I believe America has gone a long way down the wrong road. We must change roads, turn around, and go back. We must repent and commit our lives to God and to the moral and spiritual principles that have made this nation great, and

translate that commitment into action in our homes, neighborhoods, and our society. If we ever needed God's help, it is now. If we ever needed spiritual renewal, it is now. And it can begin today in each one of our lives, as we repent before God and yield ourselves to Him and His Word.

"What are you going to do?"

At the close he added, "As Ruth and I receive this award, we know that someday we will lay it at the feet of the One we seek to serve. We are deeply humbled, and we thank you for all that it represents. We pledge to continue the task that God has called us to do as long as we live."

That evening the Grahams were honored at a dinner sponsored by Memorial Mission Hospital in Asheville, North Carolina, which is depicted on the reverse side of the medal. The dinner was a benefit to launch the Graham Gold Medal Endowment for Children's Health, providing for the health needs of poor and needy children throughout the Appalachian Mountain region.

At the dinner President Bill Clinton joined Paul Harvey, Kathie Lee Gifford, and former Surgeon General C. Everett Koop in recognizing the Grahams as "two of America's finest citizens and two of the world's greatest resources."

Said the President, "I thank Billy and Ruth Graham for the ministry of their life and personal example. I thank them for countless personal gestures which indicate that as private people they are what they seem to be in public. I thank them for always doing things that will enable them to minister to people they may never know. As president, in my personal role as a citizen and a Christian, I am profoundly grateful."

Note: The above brief excerpts from Billy Graham's message were taken by permission from press accounts in the *Washington Times*, May 3, 1996, and a May 1996 issue of the *Evangelical Press News Service* report.

In an Irish pub: During a visit to Belfast, Northern Ireland, Billy goes out of his way to shake hands and make friends.

NOTES

~

INTRODUCTION

1. 1 Corinthians 1:17 (KJV).
2. Cf. Matthew 15:14.
3. Cf. Romans 3:23-24.
4. Tom Allan, *Crusade in Scotland* (London: Pickering & Inglis, 1955), 77.
5. Stanley High, *Billy Graham* (New York: McGraw Hill, 1956), 214.
6. Jeremiah 45:5 (KJV).
7. 1 Chronicles 16:22; Psalm 105:15.
8. Acts 5:34-39.
9. Cf. John 3:8.

I. THE SEED

1: THE HIGH PAGER

1. Ephesians 5:18 (KJV).
2. John Pollock, *Billy Graham* (London: Hodder & Stoughton, 1966), 62.
3. Letter from Stephen Olford, May 9, 1996. Cf. Marshall Frady, *Billy Graham* (Boston: Little, Brown, 1979); William Martin, *A Prophet with Honor* (New York: William Morrow, 1991).
4. Cf. Isaiah 55:3.
5. Cf. Acts 19:2.
6. Cf. Isaiah 55:8.

2: RESERVOIRS

1. William Martin, *A Prophet with Honor* (New York: William Morrow, 1991), 62.

3: CHALLENGE AND RESPONSE

1. William Martin, *A Prophet with Honor* (New York: William Morrow, 1991), 110.
2. John Pollock, *Billy Graham* (London: Hodder & Stoughton, 1966), 81.
3. Romans 3:4 (KJV).
4. In 1989 pilot Dwayne King of the Central Alaska Mission flew across Bering Strait with a Russian Bible and made a pioneer visit to Providentiya, Siberia. After the air traffic controller talked King's plane down to the landing strip, Dwayne led him to Christ.

4: BILLY WHO?

1. Cf. John Pollock, *Billy Graham* (London: Hodder & Stoughton, 1966), 84-91.
2. Ibid., 165.
3. Ibid., 168.
4. 1 Corinthians 14:40 (KJV).

5: THE CITY

1. Vachel Lindsay, *General William Booth Enters into Heaven and Other Poems* (New York: Macmillan, 1924), 6.
2. Warren Candler, *Great Revivals and the Great Republic* (Nashville: Methodist Episcopal Church South, Publishers, 1904), 325.
3. Isaiah 1:1-20 (KJV) formed the prophetic basis of Billy's first message in the 1958 San Francisco crusade.
4. S. E. Wirt, *Crusade at the Golden Gate* (New York: Harper & Brothers, 1959).

6: WHY ME?

1. The story of the 1959 Australian crusade is told by Stuart Barton Babbage and Ian Siggins in *Light Beneath the Cross* (Melbourne: World's Work, 1960).
2. The story of the 1959 New Zealand crusade is told by Warner Hutchinson and Cliff Wilson in *Let the People Rejoice* (Wellington, N.Z.: Crusader Bookroom Society, 1959).

7: JUST DO IT

1. Augustine's *Confessions* translated from Latin by S. E. Wirt as *Love Song* (New York: Harper & Row, 1971), 10.

8: DAKOTA DETOUR

1. A year after I left it, the newspaper ceased publication.
2. 2 Timothy 4:5 (KJV).
3. Billy Graham's weekly radio broadcast of *The Hour of Decision* continues today under direction of John Lenning.

9: IKE'S PUTTING GREEN

1. Letter in Louise Creighton, *Life of Mandell Creighton* (London: Longmans Green, 1906).
2. Sidney A. Ahlstrom, "Theology and the Present-Day Revival," *The Annals of the American Academy of the Political and Social Sciences*, November 1960.

II. THE LEAF BLADE

10: THE FIRST ISSUE

1. James Hilton, *Lost Horizon* (Boston: Houghton Mifflin, 1963).
2. At the time of my own retirement in 1976, *Decision* was published monthly in six languages: English, German, French, Spanish, Chinese (Hong Kong and Taiwan editions), and Japanese. In addition *Decision* appeared in the English language in American, British, Canadian, and Australasian editions and in Braille.
3. For information regarding the Keswick Convention Bible Conferences in England's lake country and their spread to other countries, see J. C. Pollock, *The Keswick Story* (Chicago: Moody Press, 1964).
4. Cf. John 3:30.
5. 1 Peter 1:8 (KJV).
6. 1 Corinthians 2:9.

11: THE PRAYER BASE

1. Cf. John 1:47.
2. Michael K. MacIntosh, *The Tender Touch of God* (Eugene, Ore.: Harvest House, 1996).
3. "The Lost Prayer Meeting," *Decision*, March 1973, 4.
4. So much has been written about the "Puff Graham" telegram reported to have been sent to his city editor by William Randolph Hearst, and so many different versions and denials have circulated that I withdraw from speculating. It probably did happen.
5. I have not been able to locate this quotation, but a description of a near-fatal shipwreck involving Moody and his son is found in William R. Moody, *The Life of Dwight L. Moody* (New York: Fleming H. Revell, 1900), 400ff.
6. Nehemiah 8:10.

12: BERLIN: COURAGE UNDER FIRE

1. I did not accompany the tour to Germany, being then occupied with the premier issue of *Decision*. This chapter is based on coverage that I wrote for the magazine at the time, obtained from team members who were there, from John Pollock's biography, and from contemporary German and English newspapers. I have also since visited those cities.

13: MISSING ON MOUNT SHASTA

1. William Blake, *Gnomic Verses*. See Bartlett, *Familiar Quotations* (Garden City, N.Y.: 1944), 281.
2. F. A. Iremonger, *William Temple, Archbishop of Canterbury* (London: Oxford Press, 1950).

14: WRITE THE VISION

1. As this volume indicates, my own life and ministry for Jesus Christ developed not so much through preaching or churchmanship as through writing. It is small wonder that I encourage other ministers to develop their writing skills. The San Diego County Christian Writers' Guild, which I founded in 1977, is now the largest in North America. My book *The Making of a Writer* was published by Augsburg in 1987 and in 1996 appeared in Spanish.
2. Romans 10:14.

III. THE WHEAT HEADS

15: EASTER IN BIRMINGHAM

1. I was assigned to Hamilton Field in Marin County by Fourth Air Force headquarters in San Francisco, December 1944, and reassigned to the Eleventh Air Force, Asiatic-Pacific Theater, December 1945.
2. Cf. W. P. Livingstone, *Mary Slessor of Calabar* (London: Hodder & Stoughton, 1925). See also more recent biographies.

3. This was one of the most heartening experiences of my life as we brought folks across the Golden Gate Bridge from San Francisco's Third Baptist Church every Wednesday evening to conduct services for the troops in our chapel.
4. Luke 23:34 (KJV).

16: GOD IN EARLS COURT

1. John Richard Green, *A Short History of the English People* (London: Macmillan, 1881).
2. Robert Burns, "Is There for Honest Poverty," in *Great Poems of the English Language*, ed. W. A. Briggs (New York: Tudor, 1936), 357.

17: WITH THE TROOPS IN VIETNAM

1. *Decision*, March 1969, 8.

18: WAR AND PEACE IN KOREA

1. Grady Wilson, *Count It All Joy* (Nashville: Broadman Press, 1984), 298.
2. According to my friend Rev. Billy Kim, these characterizations of Billy Graham appeared in the North Korean press and were reprinted in South Korean newspapers. Cf. John Pollock, *Billy Graham, Evangelist to the World* (New York: Harper & Row, 1979), 66. At this writing Nelson Edman (Ned) Graham, younger son of Billy and Ruth, is sending relief goods to North Korea as part of the outreach of East Gates Ministries.

19: MIRACLE IN JOHANNESBURG

1. This account, which I wrote in South Africa at the time, appeared in *Decision*, June 1973, 8.

20: ALASKA: TWO MEN PRAYED

1. This book, *Evangelism: The Next Ten Years*, was published by Word Books, Waco, Tex., in 1979.

IV. THE RIPE GRAIN

21: LEADERSHIP

1. Proverbs 16:7. In the excerpt from Cardinal Newman's speech, p. 187, he refers to this proverb as "the maxim of the ancient sage."
2. Mark 10:37.
3. Cf. Mark 10:40.
4. John 7:46.
5. Matthew 7:28-29.
6. William Martin, *A Prophet with Honor* (New York: William Morrow, 1991), 162-63.
7. Ibid., 595.
8. Cf. Ibid., 562.

9. Fred Smith, *Learning to Lead* (Dallas: Word Inc., 1986). See also "Power in Your Life," *Decision*, June 1963.

22: GREATNESS

1. William Shakespeare, *Twelfth Night*, Act 2, Scene 4.
2. Romans 5:5, my translation from the Greek.
3. Franklin P. Adams, *F. P. A.'s Book of Quotations* (New York: Funk and Wagnalls, 1952), 401.
4. Mme. Cornuel, in Bartlett, *Familiar Quotations* (Garden City, N.Y.: 1944), 1005n.
5. C. S. Lewis, *God in the Dock* (Grand Rapids: Eerdmans, 1970), 258-67.
6. J. H. Newman, *Idea of a University*, 1854 (New York: Holt, Rinehart and Winston, 1966).
7. 1 John 4:8.
8. Tom Allan, *Crusade in Scotland* (London: Pickering & Inglis, 1955), 25. At the time of Billy Graham's 1955 visit to Glasgow, Stevenson was editor of the Church of Scotland magazine, *Life and Work*.
9. Wirt & Beckstrom, *Living Quotations for Christians* (New York: Harper & Row, 1974), No. 2866.
10. Ibid., No. 1813.

23: THE ROYAL MUSKETEERS

1. 2 Samuel 23:8-11.
2. Norman P. Grubb, *C. T. Studd, Cricketer and Pioneer* (London: Lutterworth, 1949).
3. William Martin, *A Prophet with Honor* (New York: William Morrow, 1991), 573.

24: ON THE LIGHTER SIDE

1. Nehemiah 8:10.
2. Paul Rader, *Decision*, October 1963, 6-7.
3. John Pollock, *Billy Graham* (London: Hodder & Stoughton, 1966), 165-66.
4. Stanley High, *Billy Graham* (New York: McGraw Hill), 1956, 85.
5. Billy Graham, *The Secret of Happiness* (Garden City, N.Y.: Doubleday, 1955), v.
6. Billy Graham in *Decision*, June 1967 and October 1984; also in *Peace with God* (New York: Doubleday, 1953), 81.
7. Arthur Matthews, "Stroll in Cleveland," *Decision*, October 1972, 8.
8. High, *Billy Graham*, 202.
9. Dean William R. Inge, in Wirt & Beckstrom, *Living Quotations for Christians* (New York: Harper & Row, 1974), No. 1578.

V. THE HARVEST

25: THE INTERNATIONAL CONGRESSES

1. The official reports of the four international congresses are contained in the following volumes, each of which was published following the event by World Wide Publications, 1300 Harmon Place, Minneapolis, Minnesota:

Carl F. H. Henry and W. Stanley Mooneyham, eds. *One Race, One Gospel, One Task.* World Congress on Evangelism, Berlin, West Germany, October 1966, 2 vol.

J. D. Douglas, ed. *Let the Earth Hear His Voice.* International Congress on World Evangelization, Lausanne, Switzerland, July 1974.

J. D. Douglas, ed. *The Work of an Evangelist.* International Conference for Itinerant Evangelists, Amsterdam, The Netherlands, July 1983.

J. D. Douglas, ed. *The Calling of an Evangelist.* The Second International Conference for Itinerant Evangelists, Amsterdam, The Netherlands, July 1986.

26: THAWING THE COLD WAR.

1. Genesis 50:20.
2. William Martin, *A Prophet with Honor* (New York: William Morrow, 1991), 491-96.
3. This speech was delivered in Moscow, then capital of the U.S.S.R., May 11, 1982, by Dr. Graham at the world conference "Religious Workers for Saving the Sacred Gift of Life from Nuclear Catastrophe." Its text was published in full in *Christianity Today*, June 18, 1982.
4. Matthew 5:9.
5. From documents at the Billy Graham Training Center, The Cove, Asheville, North Carolina. Also from Martin, *A Prophet*, 616.
6. Telephone conversation, August 21, 1996.
7. From a national telecast aired the week of December 2, 1990, titled "Billy Graham in Eastern Europe."
8. Telephone conversation with Mr. Capen, August 21, 1996.
9. Psalm 30:5 (KJV).

27: INTO ALL THE WORLD.

1. During preparation for the Hong Kong crusade of 1975, I accompanied Robert and Karen Williams and Mrs. Ruth Graham on an excursion to Macau by hydrofoil boat. Ruth had an appointment with Rev. Luis Ruiz, a Macau missionary clergyman, and the Williamses were helping the Macau churches that wished to participate in the forthcoming crusade. We four also visited the grave of Robert Morrison (1782-1834), the British missionary who first translated the Bible into the Chinese (Cantonese) language.
2. Cf. Exodus 3:5.

APPENDIX: "THE HOPE FOR AMERICA"

1. Twenty-four years later, in 1958, Billy Graham invited that evangelist to San Francisco to take part in Billy's crusade at the Cow Palace. I was present the evening Billy introduced Rev. Mordecai F. Ham. After more than forty years, I have forgotten what the time-honored gospel warrior said, except for his opening remark: "Every day I pick up the morning paper to find out what man is going to do. Then I pick up the Bible to find out what God is going to do!"

INDEX

~